Boost Your Reading Skills

CEFR **B2**

BOOK **3**

Success
with
Reading

Maiko Ikeda

Ayaka Shimizu

Bill Benfield

Connie Sliger

JN061738

SEIBIDO

photographs

iStockphoto

音声ファイルのダウンロード／ストリーミング

CD マーク表示がある箇所は、音声を弊社 HP より無料でダウンロード／ストリーミングすることができます。下記 URL の書籍詳細ページに音声ダウンロードアイコンがございますのでそちらから自習用音声としてご活用ください。

http://seibido.co.jp/ad596

 ActeaBo

本書はテキスト連動型 Web 教材 ActeaBo に対応しています。ActeaBoでは、各 Unit に 2 編ずつ新たな英文素材が用意されており、授業で学んだリーディング方略や内容理解問題で振り返り学習することができます（本書をご利用期間中の1年間）。ActeaBo のご利用については、先生の指示に従い、ID、パスワードを取得後、下記 URL よりアクセスしてください。

http://acteabo.jp

ID	
パスワード	

※ 本サービスは教育機関におけるクラス単位でのご利用に限らせていただきます。

Success with Reading Book 3 —Boost Your Reading Skills—

Preface

Success with Reading Book 3 —Boost Your Reading Skills— is the third book of a three-volume series designed mainly to develop reading skills with the aid of learning strategies. High proficiency in English will broaden your horizons and enable you to see a more interesting world.

Each unit of *Success with Reading Book 3* follows a set structure to encourage students to put what they have learned into practice in communication activities. The unit begins with a Tips for Reading section, which introduces a strategy for more effective reading. This is followed by a Vocabulary section in which students check words related to the topic in context. They will then check their comprehension of the passage, both details and main ideas. The unit ends with opportunities for students to express and exchange their ideas regarding the related topics.

As students progress through each level, they are constantly encouraged to put what they have learned to use. At the same time, they never stop taking new challenges that will push them to a new stage. *Success with Reading Book 3* will open up a path to a place where students can look out over a wonderful landscape after enjoying every moment of the journey.

Contents

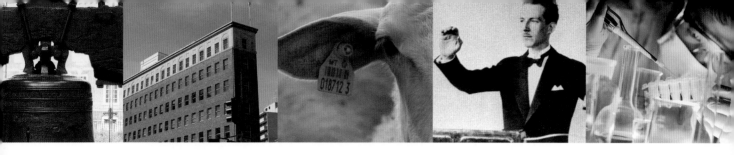

Learning Overview

KEY FOR LEARNING 1

UNIT **1** **Supporting Sentences**

Dear Diary

WARM-UP QUESTIONS

Discuss the questions below with your classmates.

1. Have you kept a diary? Why or why not?
2. Do you know any famous diary written in the past?

VOCABULARY 2

From the choices below, choose the word which fits best in each sentence.

1. When I was a child, my parents gave me a weekly _____ to buy things I wanted.
2. Joe made an _____ at the dentist's office for a regular checkup.
3. When I read a book, I always make _____ in the margin.
4. The teacher asked the students to write a _____ of the first chapter of the novel.
5. Familiarity with Internet searches is an _____ skill in both education and business.
6. Reading people's journals can provide great _____ into a particular historical period.
7. The _____ of science includes chemistry, physics, and biology.
8. It was _____ to listen to Jenny talk about her trip to Africa.
9. Having witnessed the accident, I gave a detailed _____ to the police officers.
10. The party in its new _____ was supposed to be more popular with the voters.

account	allowance	appointment	fascinating	incarnation
insights	invaluable	notations	realm	synopsis

10

---

1 **WARM-UP QUESTIONS**

Introduces warm-up questions to activate the students' background knowledge about the topic.

2 **VOCABULARY**

Teaches topic-related vocabulary words in a sentence where students can learn the usage of the words.

TIPS FOR READING

UNIT 1

Supporting Sentences (1)

Once you have got the gist from the topic sentence, you may still be anxious about not understanding the rest of the passage. It will mostly contain supporting sentences such as examples, descriptions, definitions, etc. In supporting sentences, the author gives detailed information to help convey his/her message to the reader.

Example

Scotland makes up the northern third of Great Britain and has
— topic sentence
some of the most incredible scenery in all of the United Kingdom.

If you visit Scotland's west coast, the view might seem oddly familiar to you. Why? The route taken by the Hogwarts Express in the Harry Potter movies is an actual train route in western Scotland.

— supporting sentences (examples)

EXERCISE

Check the main idea of the first paragraph on p. 12 by reading the topic sentence. Then, search for what is written in the supporting sentences.

Main idea	
Supporting idea (s)	

11

---

3 **TIPS FOR READING**

Teaches a reading strategy together with examples and key points.

EXERCISE

Provides an opportunity for using tips for reading introduced above.

4 READING PASSAGE

Features an interesting article from a variety of topics. Also, it provides an other opportunity for using tips for reading introduced in the unit.

The Diary of a Young Girl by Anne Frank on display in Germany (ph. by Rodrigo Guimba)

Anne Frank (1929—1945)

READING PASSAGE 🎧 3

Read the passage below and pay attention to the relationship between topic sentences and supporting sentences of each paragraph.

The word "diary" comes from the Latin word "diarium," which means "daily allowance." It refers to a book for fragmentary writings by date and is used for business notes, planning activities, keeping track of scheduled appointments, or documenting what has already happened. Some doctors suggest that writing in a diary is a good form of self-study.

In America, from the 1940s through the 1980s, a diary was thought of mostly as a way to privately express one's deepest thoughts while keeping notations about the day. In those times, and even continuing on today, writing in a diary was like writing to a special friend. Many times, movies would show a teenage girl beginning to write in her diary while she said aloud, "Dear diary, . . ." What followed was a synopsis of the day, usually filled with emotion.

Those private reflections may have historical significance long after the author's death. A diary kept by a young German Jewish girl by the name of Anne Frank provides us with invaluable lessons about history, for she documented her experiences while she hid from the Nazis during their occupation of the Netherlands in World War II. Her diary became one of the world's most widely read books and is the basis for many films.

Samuel Pepys, who lived during the 17th century, is the earliest diary-keeper that is famous today. His diary is also an important documentation of

12

Samuel Pepys is the earliest diary-keeper that is famous today.

history, for it gives personal insight into London's Great Plague and the Great Fire. Pepys took diary writing from the realm of business to the individual. His diary is being published on the Internet, and it is interesting to note that there has been a new entry every day since January of 2003. It will continue over the course of several years to come. Reading his diary is fascinating, and it makes his life all the more real to us.

Today's electronic version of the diary, the web log, or "blog," has once again stretched the diary to be much more than a personal account of the day's events. There are blogs to document recipes, traveling, movies, independent news, product announcements, photos, and anything else that needs to be recorded over time. Search engines like Technorati.com have been created to keep track of the more than 112 million blogs that are currently public. In its newest incarnation, the diary has become more popular than ever.

the six volumes of Samuel Pepys' diary manuscript

COMPREHENSION QUESTIONS

Decide if each statement is true [T] or false [F]. If it is false, write the sentence correctly.

1. [   ] The word "diary" means a collection of stories written every day.
2. [   ] Diary writing in movies illustrates how similar it is to writing to a special friend.
3. [   ] Anne kept a record of her private events and thoughts in her diary after she moved to Germany.
4. [   ] Pepys objectively documented details of historical events as well as his individual thoughts.
5. [   ] Today's diaries on the web are changing their characteristic of being secretive.

13

5 COMPREHENSION QUESTIONS

Introduces comprehension exercises based on the content from Reading passage.

6 GRAPHIC SUMMARY

Introduces a summary-writing exercise which is also useful as an output activity.

GRAPHIC SUMMARY

Complete the outline notes below. You can look at the passage if you want.

DIARY

1 Its origin and role
- "diary" ← Latin word "diarium"
    - = daily 1
    - = a book for 2   writing by date
- good for self-study

2 Its role in history
- a way to keep 3   about the day
- a way to privately express one's deepest 4
    have 5   significance later

    e.g. 1) Diary by Anne Frank
        provides invaluable lessons about history

    e.g. 2) Diary by Samuel Pepys (17C in London) :
        the 6   diary-keeper

        gives personal 7   into
        London's Great Plague
        the Great Fire
    ＊ being published on the Internet and
        a new 8   every day since January 2003

3 Today's version
- 9   version = the web log (or "blog")
    stretched the diary to be much more than a personal account
    = become more 10

14

7 WRITING AND DISCUSSION

Introduces questions for output exercise based on the content of the reading passage.

WRITING AND DISCUSSION

Read the questions below and write down your answers. Exchange your ideas or opinions with your classmates. Use the hints if you want.

1. Why do you think diaries have become public?

    Hints ☉ less connection / technological advancement / sharing the contents

    Your Ideas

2. If such a diary existed, whose diary would you like to read? What would you want to learn from it?

    Hints ☉ contexts / how (s)he manage / imitate

    Your Ideas

8 FURTHER STUDY

Introduces an opportunity for further independent study.

FURTHER STUDY

For further study, access ActeaBo and review today's lesson.

http://acteabo.jp

15

For successful English learning, one of the most important things is to CONTINUE learning it. You cannot master English by studying only for a couple of years. English learning is therefore very similar to climbing mountains, practicing cooking or practicing a music instrument. You need to continue.

However, you cannot continue to learn English without a CLEAR GOAL to achieve. For example, when it comes to climbing a mountain, how high is the mountain? What tools or clothes do you need for climbing? Which route are you going to take? How many days do you need? Without knowing all of this clearly, you cannot maintain your motivation and may soon give up.

Therefore, you need to set a clear goal before restarting your English learning this time. The clearer it is, the more easily you can achieve it. Also, setting SMALLER STEPS to achieve the goal helps you continue learning. Every time you take one step forward, you can feel success and the desire to move forward.

Example

Goal	Reading one passage easily without using a dictionary
Smaller steps	1. Increasing vocabulary (300 more words) 2. Reading faster ← arriving here one year later! 3. Writing a short summary (with a few sentences)

LET'S TRY

Set a clear goal for your English learning. Also, set smaller steps to achieve the goal. Do not forget to indicate where you want to be one year later through learning English with this textbook.

Goal	
Smaller steps	

UNIT **1**

Supporting Sentences

Dear Diary

WARM-UP QUESTIONS

Discuss the questions below with your classmates.

1. Have you kept a diary? Why or why not?
2. Do you know any famous diary written in the past?

VOCABULARY 2

From the choices below, choose the word which fits best in each sentence.

1. When I was a child, my parents gave me a weekly _____ to buy things I wanted.

2. Joe made an _____ at the dentist's office for a regular checkup.

3. When I read a book, I always make _____ in the margin.

4. The teacher asked the students to write a _____ of the first chapter of the novel.

5. Familiarity with Internet searches is an _____ skill in both education and business.

6. Reading people's journals can provide great _____ into a particular historical period.

7. The _____ of science includes chemistry, physics, and biology.

8. It was _____ to listen to Jenny talk about her trip to Africa.

9. Having witnessed the accident, I gave a detailed _____ to the police officers.

10. The party in its new _____ was supposed to be more popular with the voters.

account	allowance	appointment	fascinating	incarnation
insights	invaluable	notations	realm	synopsis

Supporting Sentences (1)

Once you have got the gist from the topic sentence, you may still be anxious about not understanding the rest of the passage. It will mostly contain supporting sentences such as examples, descriptions, definitions, etc. In supporting sentences, the author gives detailed information to help convey his/her message to the reader.

Example

Scotland makes up the northern third of Great Britain and has
 └─ topic sentence
some of the most incredible scenery in all of the United Kingdom.

If you visit Scotland's west coast, the view might seem oddly familiar to you. Why? The route taken by the Hogwarts Express in the Harry Potter movies is an actual train route in western Scotland.
 └─ supporting sentences (examples)

EXERCISE

Check the main idea of the first paragraph on p. 12 by reading the topic sentence. Then, search for what is written in the supporting sentences.

Main idea	
Supporting idea(s)	

DEAR DIARY
UNIT 1 · UNIT 2 · UNIT 3 · UNIT 4 · UNIT 5 · UNIT 6 · UNIT 7 · UNIT 8 · UNIT 9 · UNIT 10 · UNIT 11 · UNIT 12 · UNIT 13 · UNIT 14

11

« *The Diary of a Young Girl* by Anne Frank on display in Germany (cc by Rodrigo Galindez)

« Anne Frank
(1929–1945)

READING PASSAGE 3

Read the passage below and pay attention to the relationship between topic sentences and supporting sentences of each paragraph.

1   The word "diary" comes from the Latin word "diarium," which means "daily allowance." It refers to a book for fragmentary writings by date and is used for business notes, planning activities, keeping track of scheduled appointments, or documenting what has already happened. Some doctors suggest that writing in a
5 diary is a good form of self-study.

2   In America, from the 1940s through the 1980s, a diary was thought of mostly as a way to privately express one's deepest thoughts while keeping notations about the day. In those times, and even continuing on today, writing in a diary was like writing to a special friend. Many times, movies would show a
10 teenage girl beginning to write in her diary while she said aloud, "Dear diary, . . . " What followed was a synopsis of the day, usually filled with emotion.

3   Those private reflections may have historical significance long after the author's death. A diary kept by a young German Jewish girl by the name of Anne Frank provides us with invaluable lessons about history, for she documented
15 her experiences while she hid from the Nazis during their occupation of the Netherlands in World War II. Her diary became one of the world's most widely read books and is the basis for many films.

4   Samuel Pepys, who lived during the 17th century, is the earliest diary-keeper that is famous today. His diary is also an important documentation of history,

DEAR DIARY

UNIT 1
UNIT 2
UNIT 3
UNIT 4
UNIT 5
UNIT 6
UNIT 7
UNIT 8
UNIT 9
UNIT 10
UNIT 11
UNIT 12
UNIT 13
UNIT 14

⌄ Samuel Pepys is the earliest diary-keeper that is famous today.

20 for it gives personal insight into London's Great Plague and the Great Fire. Pepys took diary writing from the realm of business to the individual. His diary is being published on the Internet, and it is interesting to note that there has been a new entry every day since

25 January of 2003. It will continue over the course of several years to come. Reading his diary is fascinating, and it makes his life all the more real to us.

5 Today's electronic version of the diary, the web log, or "blog," has once again stretched the diary to

30 be much more than a personal account of the day's events. There are blogs to document recipes, traveling, movies, independent news, product announcements, photos, and anything else that needs to be recorded over time. Search engines like Technorati.com have

⌃ the six volumes of Samuel Pepys' diary manuscript

35 been created to keep track of the more than 112 million blogs that are currently public. In its newest incarnation, the diary has become more popular than ever.

COMPREHENSION QUESTIONS

Decide if each statement is true [T] or false [F]. If it is false, write the sentence correctly.

1. [ ] The word "diary" means a collection of stories written every day.

2. [ ] Diary writing in movies illustrates how similar it is to writing to a special friend.

3. [ ] Anne kept a record of her private events and thoughts in her diary after she moved to Germany.

4. [ ] Pepys was one of the first diary writers to include his own personal observations of historical events.

5. [ ] Today's diaries on the web are changing their characteristic of being secretive.

Complete the outline notes below. You can look at the passage if you want.

DIARY

1 Its origin and role

- "diary" ← Latin word "diarium"
    - = daily **1**
    - = a book for **2**   writing by date
- good for self-study

2 Its role in history

- a way to keep **3**   about the day
- a way to privately express one's deepest **4**
    - have **5**   significance later

    e.g. 1) Diary by Anne Frank
        provides invaluable lessons about history

    e.g. 2) Diary by Samuel Pepys (17C in London) :
            the **6**   diary-keeper

            gives personal **7**   into
                    London's Great Plague
                    the Great Fire
    * being published on the Internet and
        a new **8**   every day since January 2003

3 Today's version

- **9**   version = the web log (or "blog")
    stretched the diary to be much more than a personal account
    = become more **10**

DEAR DIARY

UNIT 1

UNIT 2
UNIT 3
UNIT 4
UNIT 5
UNIT 6
UNIT 7
UNIT 8
UNIT 9
UNIT 10
UNIT 11
UNIT 12
UNIT 13
UNIT 14

WRITING AND DISCUSSION

Read the questions below and write down your answers. Exchange your ideas or opinions with your classmates. Use the hints if you want.

1. Why do you think diaries have become public?

Hints ➡ less connection / technological advancement / sharing the contents

Your Ideas

....
....
....
....

2. If such a diary existed, whose diary would you like to read? What would you want to learn from it?

Hints ➡ contexts / how (s)he manage / imitate

Your Ideas

....
....
....
....

FURTHER STUDY

For further study, access ActeaBo and review today's lesson.

http://acteabo.jp

UNIT **2**

Supporting Sentences

Mercury

WARM-UP QUESTIONS

Discuss the questions below with your classmates.

1. What kind of metals do you know? What are they used for in our daily lives?
2. What kind of thing in nature, or pollution, are there which damages our body?

VOCABULARY 4

From the choices below, choose the word which fits best in each sentence.

1. I disagree with the widely held _____ that the economy will soon improve.
2. This drug can be _____ either as a pill or a liquid.
3. Be careful when eating mushrooms because some varieties are _____.
4. We _____ ultraviolet radiation from the sun through our skin.
5. It felt good to _____ the fresh mountain air.
6. The _____ from the burning chemicals sickened several people.
7. People must evacuate because of the imminent _____ of the volcano.
8. Microchips have several _____ in devices we use every day.
9. When setting up the shelf, make sure it is not _____ to one side.
10. The unlimited _____ of fossil fuels could lead to severe environmental damage.

| absorb | applications | assumption | eruption | exploitation |
| ingested | inhale | tilted | toxic | vapor |

Supporting Sentences (2)

Once you understand the relationship between a topic sentence and its supporting sentences, you can make a good summary. It may look like a map with landmarks (topic sentences) and details (supporting sentences).

Example

Scotland: - north + 1/3 of UK

- incredible scenery

e.g.) west coast = Harry Potter movies!

EXERCISE

Make notes for a summary of Paragraph 1 of the passage on p. 18. First, pick up a few key words from the topic sentences. Then, add some more key words from the supporting sentences.

Summary of Paragraph 1

>> mercury

Read the passage below and pay attention to supporting sentences.

1   Mercury is one of the first metals to be discovered by humans; the earliest known use dates to the pyramids of Egypt, about 1500 years BCE. Much mysticism and erroneous assumptions have surrounded it throughout the centuries, probably due to the fact that it is liquid at room temperature. In 210
5 BCE, the Chinese emperor Qin Shi Huang died from ingesting a mercury-laden concoction that was intended to make him immortal. The forebears of modern chemistry, the alchemists, believed that mercury was the common base of all metals and that one could make any metal by adding other substances to it. Mercury was even used, unsuccessfully, to treat syphilis for at least 400 years.

10 **2**   Mercury is not needed by, nor is it useful to, the human body or any other living organism in any way, as once thought. In fact, it is extremely toxic and causes a number of severe problems. One of the easiest ways for the body to absorb mercury is by inhaling the vapors. Half of the mercury pollution that is now in the air comes from natural sources, such as volcanic eruptions. The
15 other half is mostly the result of burning coal to produce electricity. It is very difficult for the human body to remove mercury using its own defenses or even for doctors to remove it by chelation, making it critical that exposure to mercury always be kept to an extreme minimum. Despite these facts, it is still used in a number of ways that bring it into intimate contact with humans, such
20 as dental fillings, vaccine preservatives, cosmetics, and several ingested and

>> vaccine

>> vapor

⌃ Half of the mercury pollution comes from natural sources, such as volcanic eruptions.

UNIT 1

MERCURY

UNIT 2

UNIT 3

UNIT 4

UNIT 5

UNIT 6

UNIT 7

UNIT 8

UNIT 9

UNIT 10

UNIT 11

UNIT 12

UNIT 13

UNIT 14

topical medications.

3 Today, most people see mercury used in lighting applications. It is in fluorescent bulbs, television picture tubes, mercury-vapor lamps, neon signs, and tilt switches. It was once commonly used in thermometers and blood
25 pressure meters, but the high potential for poisoning has nearly eliminated such use. Mercury is also employed in the extraction of gold and silver from mined dirt and in several other industrial processes. A rather fascinating function is in telescopes, where a six meter diameter tray is slowly rotated, causing the metal to form a perfectly parabolic mirror.

30 **4** As more people become aware of the dangers of mercury, its exploitation has become moderated and more carefully controlled. Balancing caution and technological applications is making mercury a contentious element.

Mercury is used in a number of ways:

➤ dental filling   ➤ neon signs   ➤ thermometer

COMPREHENSION QUESTIONS

Decide if each statement is true [T] or false [F]. If it is false, write the sentence correctly.

1. [   ] It was once believed that mercury could change any metal into liquid.

2. [   ] The human activity of generating electricity creates mercury air pollution.

3. [   ] Once taken into the human body, mercury is difficult to remove even by medical treatment.

4. [   ] Mercury is not found in tooth fillings because of its risk of intimate contact with the human body.

5. [   ] The use of mercury in thermometers has been encouraged after its poisonous nature was eliminated.

Complete the outline notes below. You can look at the passage if you want.

MERCURY

1 History
- about 1500 BCE   first metal discovered by humans (in Egypt)
- 210 BCE   Qin Shi Huang died from ingesting

  a mercury-laden concoction

  intended to make him 1
- believed to be the common base of all metals

  = possible to make any metal by adding other 2   to it
- even used to 3   syphilis for at least 400 years

2 Toxic features
- causes many severe problems
- by 4   the vapors

  from natural sources   e.g.) volcanic eruptions

  from burning 5
- difficult to 6   for the human body

  for doctors

STILL
- used in many ways to bring it into intimate contact with humans

  e.g.) dental fillings,   vaccine 7   ,

  cosmetics,   ingested and topical medications

3 Its application today
- used in lighting 8

  e.g.) fluorescent bulbs,   television picture tubes,

  mercury-vapor lamps,   neon signs,   tilt switches

  * nearly 9   from thermometers and blood

  pressure meters
- employed in the 10   of gold and silver
- functions in telescopes: forms a parabolic mirror

- being aware of its dangers → its exploitation becoming more

  moderate and more controlled

WRITING AND DISCUSSION

Read the questions below and write down your answers. Exchange your ideas or opinions with your classmates. Use the hints if you want.

1. Do you think exploitation of mercury is acceptable or not? Why?

Hints ➡ useful / identified / safety

> **Your Ideas**
>
> ....
>
> ....
>
> ....
>
> ....

2. Can you think of some things that were once commonly used but are not used any more?

Hints ➡ negative impact / disappeared / widespread

> **Your Ideas**
>
> ....
>
> ....
>
> ....
>
> ....

FURTHER STUDY

For further study, access ActeaBo and review today's lesson.

http://acteabo.jp

Paying attention to discourse markers

Swine Flu

WARM-UP QUESTIONS

Discuss the questions below with your classmates.

1. What kind of seasonal diseases do you have? What are your symptoms?
2. What do you usually do to protect yourself from influenza?

VOCABULARY 🎧 6

From the choices below, choose the word which fits best in each sentence.

1. The _____ of the local park as a disaster evacuation zone has just been confirmed.

2. "_____" is an old-fashioned word for "pig" and is now used only in specialized expressions.

3. _____ skeletons differ in many respects from those of mammals.

4. In 2020, a new type of corona virus caused a global _____.

5. The number of super typhoons last year was _____.

6. The collapse of the pedestrian bridge caused several hundred _____.

7. The traffic accident was _____ to a combination of icy roads and fog.

8. _____ sufferers often carry an inhaler, which is a device that helps them breathe.

9. The _____ company announced the introduction of a new drug to treat diabetes.

10. Nowadays, we have a _____ of online entertainment options.

asthma	attributed	avian	casualties	designation
pandemic	pharmaceutical	plethora	swine	unprecedented

Paying attention to discourse markers (1)

Discourse markers help us better understand the structure of a passage. Reading without these words is like walking in the forest without any signs. Below are some examples of useful discourse markers.

Example

Contrastive	but, however, nevertheless
Inferential	therefore, then
Ordering	first, next, then, second, finally
Cause / Effect	because, due to

EXERCISE

Highlight the discourse markers in Paragraphs 1 and 2 of the passage on p. 24. Try using them to understand the structure of the passage.

	Discourse markers	Structure of the paragraph
Paragraph 1		
Paragraph 2		

Read the passage below and pay attention to discourse markers.

1   The scientific designation H1N1, known as the Swine Flu virus, is a seasonal influenza that normally only affects pigs. Occasionally, an animal-related virus infects humans, such as the Avian Flu, but this is rare, because it is very difficult for humans to be infected by animal viruses.

5 **2**   The current H1N1 scare may be history repeating: in 1976, the United States Centers for Disease Control had a huge campaign to immunize everyone in the country against the upcoming Swine Flu pandemic. Thousands of people were immunized against the killer disease, as the news outlets warned of unprecedented suffering and mass casualties. In a most telltale turn of

10 events, the following happened: one person died from Swine Flu; 25 died and thousands were injured by the Swine Flu vaccine's side-effects, including paralysis, Guillain-Barré syndrome, and other neuromuscular and auto-immune disorders, with the government paying for damages.

3   According to the World Health Organization, by January, 2010, there had

15 been roughly 12,220 deaths attributed to H1N1 worldwide and the worst had passed. While this may seem like a large number, when put into context, H1N1 becomes almost insignificant, since 250,000 to 500,000 people die from the ordinary seasonal flu each year. The vast majority of the deaths caused by the Swine Flu were in people who already had health problems, such as asthma

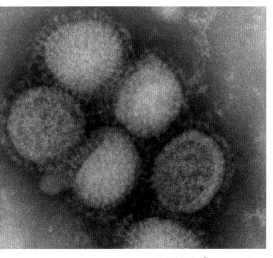

⌃ H1N1 influenza virus

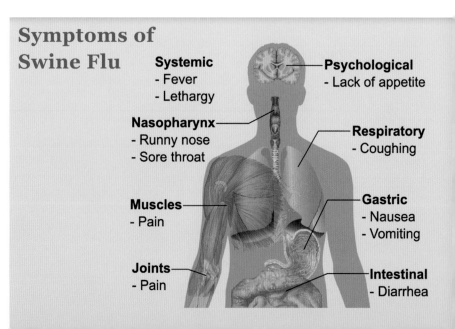

Symptoms of Swine Flu

Systemic
- Fever
- Lethargy

Psychological
- Lack of appetite

Nasopharynx
- Runny nose
- Sore throat

Respiratory
- Coughing

Muscles
- Pain

Gastric
- Nausea
- Vomiting

Joints
- Pain

Intestinal
- Diarrhea

UNIT 1

UNIT 2

SWINE FLU

UNIT 3

UNIT 4

UNIT 5

UNIT 6

UNIT 7

UNIT 8

UNIT 9

UNIT 10

UNIT 11

UNIT 12

UNIT 13

UNIT 14

20 and immune disorders. Most of the people who have lived through it report that it behaves very much like an ordinary flu, but with milder symptoms.

4 The reason that the Swine Flu is being exaggerated is unclear. Perhaps it's precautionary, but history indicates that exaggerated precautions are unnecessary. The more likely answer may be one that applies to much of

25 human nature: easy profits. The news media get more attention when they prophesy doom and gloom. Also on the "gravy train" are the pharmaceutical companies who make the H1N1 tests, the H1N1 vaccines, and a plethora of anti-viral drugs. The more that people become frightened, the more they demand a response from their governments to protect them. Corporate profits

30 become much easier when the government is the buyer.

5 How the pathogen jumped from farm animals to humans is not known, but it is known that eating pork products does not put one at risk. The virus is most likely spread through human contact, but it is not easily transmitted through the air. However, for the most protection, it may be recommended in

35 some places that the public take precautions by wearing a mask along with the everyday measures one takes to avoid the ordinary, seasonal flu, such as frequent hand washing.

COMPREHENSION QUESTIONS

Decide if each statement is true [T] or false [F]. If it is false, write the sentence correctly.

1. [   ] Different from the Avian Flu, the Swine Flu virus can infect humans.

2. [   ] People in the US were immunized to protect them from dying from Swine Flu.

3. [   ] The symptoms of Swine Flu are very similar to those of seasonal influenza.

4. [   ] Exaggeration of the Swine Flu is likely due to people's tendency to want to make profits easily.

5. [   ] In addition to usual precautions for seasonal flu, people are sometimes advised to wear a mask.

Complete the outline notes below. You can look at the passage if you want.

SWINE FLU

1 Effect on humans?
- H1N1 = scientific designation
- rare for animal-related virus (e.g., the **1** _____ Flu) to infect humans

  ∴ difficult for humans to be infected by animal viruses

2 History repeating
- 1976 in the US

  huge campaign to **2** _____ everyone against the

  3 _____ Swine Flu

  → 1 _____ died from Swine Flu

   25 _____ died from its vaccine's **4**

   thousands injured by its vaccine's **4** _____

3 Statistics in context
- by January 2010   roughly 12,220 deaths worldwide

   - almost **5**

    ∴ 250,000 to 500,000 deaths

      from **6** _____ seasonal flu each year
   - mostly already had health problems

4 Reasons for exaggeration
- unclear: perhaps **7** _____ ← unnecessary

   : probably easy profit

      = - more attention on the news media by

       8 _____ doom and gloom
      - more people frightened

      → more **9** _____ for government responses
      → the government buys more H1N1 tests, vaccines, and anti-viral drugs

      → more profits to **10** _____ companies

5 Ways of infection
- unknown: NOT by eating pork products

   : most likely through human contact

WRITING AND DISCUSSION

Read the questions below and write down your answers. Exchange your ideas or opinions with your classmates. Use the hints if you want.

1. How would you protect yourself from Swine Flu?

> **Hints** ➡ constant exercise / keep one's immunity / reliable information

> Your Ideas
> ....
> ....
> ....
> ....
> ....

2. If you face the frightening possibility of catching an infectious disease, what would you demand from the government?

> **Hints** ➡ wages / reliable Wi-Fi service / receive accurate information

> Your Ideas
> ....
> ....
> ....
> ....
> ....

FURTHER STUDY

For further study, access ActeaBo and review today's lesson.

http://acteabo.jp

SWINE FLU

UNIT 1
UNIT 2
UNIT 3
UNIT 4
UNIT 5
UNIT 6
UNIT 7
UNIT 8
UNIT 9
UNIT 10
UNIT 11
UNIT 12
UNIT 13
UNIT 14

Getting a Good Night's Sleep

WARM-UP QUESTIONS

Discuss the questions below with your classmates.

1. How many hours do you sleep at night on average?

2. What do you usually do two hours prior to going to sleep?

VOCABULARY 🔘 8

From the choices below, choose the word which fits best in each sentence.

1. I plan to buy an old house and _____ it before moving in.

2. Because of my _____, I sleep only about three hours a night on average.

3. If you are feeling down, the best _____ is fresh air and exercise.

4. Bob felt great _____ at the prospect of losing his job.

5. The gas explosion created _____ in the downtown area.

6. Joe has a strong _____ system and can eat any kind of food with no problem.

7. My cold is causing _____ in my nose.

8. _____ is the inability to breathe properly when sleeping.

9. Frank's injuries are so serious that he will have to stay in the hospital _____.

10. We will immediately _____ the wrong order we sent you.

apnea	congestion	digestive	distress	havoc
indefinitely	insomnia	rectify	refurbish	remedy

Paying attention to discourse markers (2)

When you read with a focus on conjunctions and conjunctive adverbs, you can more easily understand the storyline of a passage. Then, you can take good notes by using symbols and abbreviations. Here is an example of notes from Paragraph 3, Unit 3.

Example

January 2020 :

    about 12,220 deaths from H1N1 worldwide (according to WHO)

        - seem like a large number

            BUT

        insignificant in context

        - mostly people who already had health problems

          e.g.) asthma, immune disorders

EXERCISE

Take notes for Paragraph 1 of the passage on p. 30 paying attention to discourse markers. Then, compare your notes with your classmates.

>> Your body must refurbish itself by getting enough good sleep.

READING PASSAGE CD 9

Read the passage below and pay attention to discourse markers.

1 Your body must refurbish itself by getting enough good sleep in order to stay healthy. Moreover, daytime sleepiness can negatively affect your work, studies, relationships, and socioeconomic condition. The purpose of this article is to help you to understand what may be going on when you
5 experience insomnia and to offer some simple remedies that may save you from unnecessary distress.

2 Sometimes, when your schedule changes, for instance, your body needs a period of adjustment of a week or two. At other times, you may have been too physically active right before bedtime and made yourself wide awake. It is
10 good to exercise every day for 30 minutes, but not close to bedtime.

3 Another way that you may become wide awake late at night is by being too mentally active. Do not do your work or watch television in bed, but instead give yourself about a two-hour period of calm. It might be beneficial to keep a personal journal. In this way, you can write down the problems you
15 may need to address the following day. It is better to write them down than to lie awake thinking about them.

4 Take a hot shower or bath, or visit the sauna as a way of getting ready

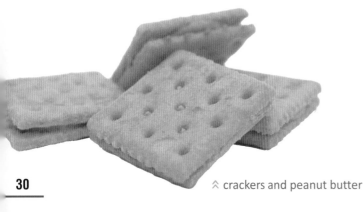

⌃ crackers and peanut butter

⌃ Caffeine may cause insomnia.

⌄ Take a hot bath as a way of getting ready for bed.

for bed. When your body's temperature is raised at night, it will fall at bedtime,

20 assisting you in falling asleep. Go to the bathroom before going to bed, so that it is less likely that you'll have to get up during the night.

5 It is important to know what to

25 avoid eating, for certain things can cause havoc in your digestive system and keep you awake. Allergies to foods cause congestion and stomach upset, and being too full can cause sleep apnea. Caffeine may cause insomnia if you consume it in the afternoon, because it does not metabolize efficiently. In addition, do not drink alcohol before bed,

30 because it keeps you from sleeping deeply. What is best, however, is to eat a small portion of high-protein food several hours before bedtime, such as a small plate of crackers and peanut butter, for this helps the essential amino acid, L-tryptophan, to produce melatonin, a hormone that controls sleep.

6 Sleeplessness can be a matter of one night, or it may go on indefinitely. It

35 is good to remember how to rectify the situation so that you are not anxious about not getting enough rest for the next day's challenges.

COMPREHENSION QUESTIONS

Decide if each statement is true [T] or false [F]. If it is false, write the sentence correctly.

1. [ ] Poor sleep can bring negative results in social behavior as well as work.

2. [ ] Taking a bath helps you sleep smoothly because it helps your temperature drop.

3. [ ] Keeping a journal can help expose your negative feelings and get rid of them.

4. [ ] Eating large amounts of food can cause sleep apnea.

5. [ ] Alcohol can make it difficult for you to wake up as it causes you to sleep very deeply.

Complete the outline notes below. You can look at the passage if you want.

DOS AND DON'TS FOR GOOD NIGHT'S SLEEP

1 Purpose of the article

- helps readers understand what is 1
- offers some simple remedies for unnecessary 2

2 Physical

o 30-minute exercise every day (× not 3   to bedtime)

3 Mental

× work in bed

× watch television in bed

o a two-hour period of 4

4 Others

o take a hot shower or bath

o visit the sauna

∵ body 5   raised at night → fall at bedtime

→ assist in falling asleep

o go to the bathroom before bed

5 Dietary

× allergies to foods (→ 6   and stomach upset)

× too full (→ sleep 7   )

× caffeine in the afternoon (→ 1   )

× alcohol before bed (→ not sleep deeply)

o a small 8   of high- 9   food several
hours before bedtime

∵ the essential amino 10   (= L-tryptophan) produces
melatonin a hormone to control sleep

UNIT 1
UNIT 2
UNIT 3
UNIT 4
UNIT 5
UNIT 6
UNIT 7
UNIT 8
UNIT 9
UNIT 10
UNIT 11
UNIT 12
UNIT 13
UNIT 14

GETTING A GOOD NIGHT'S SLEEP

WRITING AND DISCUSSION

Read the questions below and write down your answers. Exchange your ideas or opinions with your classmates. Use the hints if you want.

1. Suppose you had just arrived in the UK in the evening after a long flight from Japan. What would you do to have a good night's sleep?

Hints ➲ relax / release stress / stretch

> Your Ideas
>
> ....
> ....
> ....
> ....
> ....

2. What kind of environment do you think would make it easy for you to sleep?

Hints ➲ pillow / darkness / prevent

> Your Ideas
>
> ....
> ....
> ....
> ....
> ....

FURTHER STUDY

ActeaBo

For further study, access ActeaBo and review today's lesson.

http://acteabo.jp

Fact or Opinion

Paul Gauguin

WARM-UP QUESTIONS

Discuss the questions below with your classmates.

1. Who are some of the famous painters or artists you know well?
2. In which form do you like to express your feelings, for example, playing a musical instrument, dancing, etc.?

VOCABULARY 🎧 10

From the choices below, choose the word which fits best in each sentence.

1. Galileo is often _____ with inventing the telescope, but that is not entirely true.
2. As well as paintings, we saw many beautiful _____ in the art gallery.
3. The _____ colors of the flowers gave the room a joyful feeling.
4. My younger brother's _____ with video games is affecting his schoolwork.
5. Japanese restaurants sometimes have _____ meals in display cases outside.
6. When eating French food, it is _____ to have cheese before the dessert.
7. Many people are _____ with the government's response to climate change.
8. The fire _____ for several hours before the firefighters could extinguish it.
9. I feel a _____ to buy books whenever I pass by a bookstore.
10. The executive was punished for his illegal dealings by _____ of three months' salary.

artificial	blazed	compulsion	conventional	credited
discontented	forfeiture	obsession	sculptures	vibrant

34

Fact or Opinion (1)

Most pieces of writing contain a mixture of facts and opinions. By differentiating these two, you can more deeply understand the contents. Facts are things that can be proved to be true — whether it be through tests, records, or documents — while opinions express the author's beliefs or judgements.

Example

Fact	According to *Newsweek*, the best university in the world is Harvard University.
Opinion	Being a highly skilled reader is the key to becoming successful in the Information Age.

EXERCISE

Read the following sentences and decide which is fact and which is opinion.

A: Soccer fans are very serious about the sport they love, and some of them feel that their soccer team is just as important as their country.

B: In 1969, El Salvador and Honduras fought a four-day war after a FIFA World Cup qualifying match.

Sentence	Your Answer		
Sentence A	**fact**	or	**opinion**
Sentence B	**fact**	or	**opinion**

READING PASSAGE 11

Read the passage below and pay attention to the differences of fact and opinion.

1   Paul Gauguin (1848–1903) is one of the famous French painters of the Post-Impressionist movement. He is credited with producing over 150 paintings and sculptures, many of which have a vibrant, tropical theme. His masterpieces include *Vision After the Sermon* (1888) and *Tahitian Women on*
5 *the Beach* (1891).

2   Gauguin started life as a merchant marine and stockbroker. Despite chances at a solid career, passion for his painting hobby soon became an obsession. Even his friends were painters, and he spent time socially
10 and painted with them as well. The impressive list includes Pissarro, Cézanne, Monet, and Van Gogh.

3   In an effort to distance himself from what he perceived as an artificial and conventional influence in Paris, Gauguin moved to Martinique, an island north
15 of South America, and created perhaps 12 paintings there. Unfortunately, he suffered from illnesses common to tropical areas in poverty: dysentery and malaria. Nonetheless, a few years later, he moved to Tahiti in the equatorial Pacific, where he backed the
20 natives against the occupying French government and the Catholic Church. His art became progressively more primitive in Tahiti and made greater use of

⌄ *Tahitian Women on the Beach* (1891)

⌃ *Vision After the Sermon* (1888)

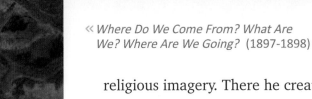

religious imagery. There he created his most famous painting, *Where Do We Come
From? What Are We? Where Are We Going?*

25 **4**   The Post-Impressionist movement that Paul Gauguin affected heavily is defined
by what it is not, and for good reason. He and other French painters who felt
discontented with the weaknesses of the Impressionistic style, such as insignificant
subject matter and lack of structure, blazed paths through an unexplored, artistic
wilderness. Gauguin's work countered the shortcomings of Impressionism, making
30 liberal use of symbolism, nearly eliminating customary perspective and balancing
color and form equally. He focused on conveying a thought and virtually ruled
out everything inconsequential to that thought. In the words of a current French
artist by the name of Bérengère Sudmann, who has been influenced and moved by
Gauguin's works, " . . . a painting by Gauguin often tells (and reveals) much more
35 than a good photo today."

5   Looking at Paul Gauguin's personal life, you will find that his compulsion for
painting played a big part in his forfeiture of everything else important. In the end,
he had sacrificed life with his wife and five children, his homeland, his health, and,
eventually, his very own existence. He suffered from depression in spite of his great
40 talent and allowed himself to become an alcoholic. Paul Gauguin died from syphilis
at only 54 years old and rests in the Marquesas Islands.

COMPREHENSION QUESTIONS

*Decide if each statement is true [T] or false [F]. If it is false, write
the sentence correctly.*

1. [   ] Gauguin is famous for his works featuring tropical images
    with bright colors.

2. [   ] After failure in his previous business, Gauguin started his
    career as an artist.

3. [   ] Gauguin left Paris in order to escape from the criticism of his
    paintings as artificial.

4. [   ] Gauguin supported the locals in Tahiti in resisting the power
    of French government and the Catholic Church.

5. [   ] As a Post-Impressionist painter, Gauguin emphasized
    expressing only one thought in his paintings.

Complete the outline notes below. You can look at the passage if you want.

PORTRAIT OF PAUL GAUGUIN

1 Overview
- famous Post-Impressionist French painter (1848-1903)
- produced over 150 paintings and sculptures

2 Start as an artist
- a 1   marine and stockbroker
- painting as hobby → obsessed
  * artist friends : Pissarro, Cézanne, Monet, Van Gogh

3 Leaving Paris
- to 2   from "artificial and 3   " influence
  → Martinique: created 12 paintings
        : suffered from illnesses
  → Tahiti : against the occupying French government and the
        4   Church
      : progressively more 5
      : made greater use of 6   imagery

4 In Post-Impressionist movement
  : 7   with the weakness of the Impressionistic style
  : making liberal use of symbolism
  : 8   customary perspective
  : balancing color and form equally
  : focused on conveying a thought

5 Personal life
- 9   of everything else important
  ← 10   for painting

WRITING AND DISCUSSION

Read the questions below and write down your answers. Exchange your ideas or opinions with your classmates. Use the hints if you want.

1. Would you like to make a living from your own hobby? Why or why not?

Hints ➲ occupy / lifetime / gradually dislike

Your Ideas

....
....
....
....
....

2. Do you want to live as Gauguin did? Why or why not?

Hints ➲ devotion / abandon / sacrifice

Your Ideas

....
....
....
....
....

FURTHER STUDY

ActeaBo

For further study, access ActeaBo and review today's lesson.

http://acteabo.jp

UNIT 1
UNIT 2
UNIT 3
UNIT 4
UNIT 5
PAUL GAUGUIN
UNIT 6
UNIT 7
UNIT 8
UNIT 9
UNIT 10
UNIT 11
UNIT 12
UNIT 13
UNIT 14

UNIT **6** **Fact or Opinion**

Bicycle Fever

WARM-UP QUESTIONS

Discuss the questions below with your classmates.

1. What sports do you like to do most?

2. If you visit a city for sightseeing, which form of transportation do you prefer to use? Why?

VOCABULARY   CD 12

From the choices below, choose the word which fits best in each sentence.

1. Greenhouse gas _____ pose a threat to the earth's climate.

2. An apartment block will be built on the vacant _____ next to my house.

3. Living in the mountains is a _____ as far as my family's health is concerned.

4. The band's popularity _____ after they released one disappointing song after another.

5. It was hard work riding my bicycle up the steep _____.

6. My sister is an _____ hiker and goes to the mountains every weekend.

7. My mother _____ to me that she would be coming to visit this weekend.

8. The Harry Potter books _____ an interest in reading among children and teenagers.

9. _____ with people from other countries will boost your cultural awareness.

10. Recently there has been an increase in newspaper _____ about self-driving cars.

articles	avid	blessing	ebbed	emissions
engagement	incline	lot	mentioned	spurred

Fact or Opinion (2)

Authors' opinions can be reflected in their choice of adjectives. Paying attention to these adjectives helps you better understand the authors' ideas.

Example

Fact	Glass is made from sand.
Opinion	Glass is a beautiful kind of art.

EXERCISE

Read the passage below and mark facts and opinions as in the example given.

> One of the most amazing sights of Yellowstone National Park is Old
>   opinion
> Faithful, a cone geyser. Although it is not the tallest or the largest,
> it is the most famous of the almost 10,000 natural springs and
> geysers in the national park. The spectacular geyser shoots boiling
> hot water over 50 meters into the air about every one and a half
> hours. Though its average interval of eruptions has lengthened over
> the years, Old Faithful is still as fantastic and predictable as it was a
> century ago.

Read the passage below and pay attention to the differences of fact and opinion.

>> cyclist

1 The bicycle has been a commonplace mode of transportation around the world for many years. It will never become a thing of the past because of its many advantages: it is good for
5 the environment, for there are no toxic emissions with vehicles that are man-powered; it is very good for your health, for pedaling is good aerobic and muscle tone exercise, and not having to look for a parking place in crowded lots is always a
10 blessing. Being able to go off-road on dirt bikes makes it a favorite sport.

2 As in all activities, bicycle riding has had its ebb and flow. Recently, however, since about 2002, there has been such an enthusiastic incline
15 that it's now being called "bicycle fever." In the United States in 2005, for example, bicycle sales exceeded that of new cars and trucks combined. Most credit it to those who want to "go green" and save the planet when they bike rather than
20 drive a car, but there is another reason: the specialized bicycles on the market, along with all the gear that goes with them, have made casual touring, mountain trail riding, and dirt biking very attractive to all age groups. It is when avid
25 cyclists have exceeded the limits of their previous bicycling habits that they may go on to join what some think of as the "elite" group of bicycling—

>> bicycle racing

UNIT 1
UNIT 2
UNIT 3
UNIT 4
UNIT 5
UNIT 6
BICYCLE FEVER
UNIT 7
UNIT 8
UNIT 9
UNIT 10
UNIT 11
UNIT 12
UNIT 13
UNIT 14

« bicycle helmet

bicycle racing. Usually, it is with great pains, however, that they purchase bicycles for

30 racing, because each can cost over $1,500.

3 All of this rather elaborate, and not to mention expensive, bicycle paraphernalia spurs on a great number of bicycle-centered activities and events; thus, you should know the "rules of

35 engagement," so to speak. With a little research, you can find countless articles on bicycle safety and etiquette. If you join a tour with a group of cyclists, which is a good, up-close way to see new sights, your tour guide will go over the rules of the road for you.

4 From the earliest bicycle, the high-wheeler, to racing bicycles

40 today, we have indeed come a long way. (Just imagine mounting a bicycle where the seat was several feet up and the wheels were made of wood!) What does not change over time is that cycling has been, and will continue to be, both sporty and entertaining for us.

COMPREHENSION QUESTIONS

Decide if each statement is true [T] or false [F]. If it is false, write the sentence correctly.

1. [   ] Some people enjoy riding a bicycle on rough ground.

2. [   ] Bicycle riding was popular in every generation in the past.

3. [   ] Many people in the US purchased used bicycles to save the planet in 2005.

4. [   ] Production of elaborate and specialized bicycles has led to an increase in bicycle-related events.

5. [   ] The seats of the earliest bicycles were at high above waist level.

Complete the outline notes below. You can look at the passage if you want.

CYCLING AS A POPULAR SPORT

1 Advantages
- good for the environment
    - ∵ man- **1**   and no **2**   emission
- good for your health
    - ∵ good aerobic and **3**   tone exercise
- no need to look for a parking place in crowded **4**

2 Bicycle fever
- since about 2002
    - e.g.) 2005 in the US

        bicycles **5**   >   **5**   of new
                                      cars and trucks

    - ∵ - more people want to "go green"
    - specialized bicycles on the market
        - → all age groups **6**   to casual touring
                               mountain trail riding
                               dirt biking
- when **7**   the limit of previous bicycling habits
    - → join bicycle racing
        - ∗ BUT! with great **8**   of purchasing costly bicycles for racing

3 To more activities and events
- **9**   (and expensive) paraphernalia
    - → a great number of bicycle-centered activities and events
    - → better to know the "rules of **10**   "
                    = on bicycle safety and etiquette
        - by reading articles
        - by joining a cycling tour

UNIT 1
UNIT 2
UNIT 3
UNIT 4
UNIT 5
BICYCLE FEVER
UNIT 6
UNIT 7
UNIT 8
UNIT 9
UNIT 10
UNIT 11
UNIT 12
UNIT 13
UNIT 14

WRITING AND DISCUSSION

Read the questions below and write down your answers. Exchange your ideas or opinions with your classmates. Use the hints if you want.

1. Do you want to use a bicycle to travel from your house to the nearest station or campus? Why or why not?

   Hints ➡ save time / hills / tired

   > Your Ideas
   >
   > ....
   > ....
   > ....
   > ....

2. Suppose you and your team were in charge of the campaign of "Enjoy Cycling" at university. How would you involve more students in the campaign and have them actively participate in it?

   Hints ➡ attract / discuss / cooperate

   > Your Ideas
   >
   > ....
   > ....
   > ....
   > ....

FURTHER STUDY

For further study, access ActeaBo and review today's lesson.

http://acteabo.jp

UNIT **7** **Summarizing**

In the Spirit of Suomi — Finland's Cultural Industry

WARM-UP QUESTIONS

Discuss the questions below with your classmates.

1. What is your resource for everyday news?

2. Do you watch TV or listen to the radio? Why or why not?

VOCABULARY 🎵 14

From the choices below, choose the word which fits best in each sentence.

1. It always makes me happy when I see the sea _____ in the bright sunshine.

2. Most plants will not _____ if they do not get enough sunshine.

3. American English is _____ from British English in its vocabulary and spelling.

4. The city plans to launch several new _____ to boost tourism.

5. The revised tax laws will make it easier for people to launch new _____.

6. The college offers a whole _____ of courses, from science to liberal arts.

7. My _____ interests are mainly limited to 19th and 20th century novels.

8. I was chosen to _____ my university at a national speech contest.

9. Although my height is only 1.65 meters, in my family I am _____ tall.

10. If these poor economic trends continue, the economy will likely fall into _____.

comparatively	distinct	endeavors	enterprises	literary
recession	represent	sparkle	spectrum	thrive

Summarizing (1)

You have now understood the structure of a paragraph (Units 1 and 2), the storyline of a passage with discourse markers (Units 3 and 4), and how to distinguish between fact and opinion (Units 5 and 6). As a next step, it is also effective to briefly summarize each paragraph of a passage. In summarizing you can reflect on what you have just read and check how well you understand the paragraph. This process also helps you keep the information you obtained longer in your memory and acquire it as new knowledge.

EXERCISE

Summarize each paragraph of the passage below. Then, check if there is any new information to you in them.

> Many people think of sharks as evil, man-eating monsters that hunt innocent swimmers down to attack and devour them. This image is far from the truth, however, and has largely been constructed by Hollywood movie producers who use this false impression to add an element of fear and danger to their movies.
>
> In fact, many shark species are not predators at all, but are scavengers who feed on already dead prey. Out of over 470 shark species, only four have been involved in a significant number of fatal attacks on humans: the great white shark, oceanic whitetip shark, tiger shark, and bull shark. These four huge, powerful species are capable of inflicting serious injuries on their victims. However, these species usually avoid contact with humans as we are not a part of their natural diet. The average number of fatal shark attacks per year is about four, and if you compare this to the number of sharks killed each year by humans — over 100 million — it is the sharks who should be scared of us, not the other way around.

Summary

READING PASSAGE   15

Read the passage below and summarize it.

1   One may never guess that a land filled with green forests, sparkling lakes, and old castles would lie at the Arctic Circle and boast a thriving cultural industry as well. Such is the case of Finland. The Finns call it Suomi—"land of lakes and marshes," and from Suomi is born a creativity that is their pride.

5   **2**   The term "cultural industry" refers to a distinct collection of successful and/or profitable endeavors that have to do with the culture of a given area or country. One reason that the cultural industry of Finland is thriving is because of its early beginnings in the 1700s and the time that it has had to evolve. From 2000 to 2005, however, it grew faster than other types of commercial

10   enterprises due to an increase in leisure time of the consumer. What makes Finland's cultural industry noteworthy is that it has gone on to become greater than that of forestry in this northern, tree-covered area.

3   The citizens of Finland take time to satisfy their interest

15   in the world around them by way of their country's newspapers.

>> Newspaper publishing is Finland's
largest cultural industry.

>> broadcasting

Newspaper publishing is Finland's largest cultural industry with over 100 distributed nationally. Local and national broadcasting broaden the spectrum of possibilities in the ways to spend free time, and so it is not surprising that broadcasting has taken

20 second place. It is interesting that while radio broadcasting is on the national level, television broadcasting is handled locally because of a public desire for decentralization.

4   Book publishing is third on the list of Finland's cultural industries, with about 600 literary societies representing book publishing companies. It is an amazing fact

25 that given its comparatively remote location, climate, and low population density and growth rate, Finland had the world's largest per capita production of books until the 1980s, a relatively recent time in history. It is also fascinating to learn how alive Swedish language literature is in Finland. Books by Swedish authors are a main focus at the annual Helsinki Book Fair, an event that showcases the very

30 essence of Finland's literary culture, stretching for four full days and featuring a wide range of subjects from science to the latest "e-book."

5   In today's global economy, there is optimism about Finland's ability to weather possible recessions. This is no surprise, for in Suomi, the Finnish creative spirit in its cultural industry will always help to see it through.

COMPREHENSION QUESTIONS
Decide if each statement is true [T] or false [F]. If it is false, write the sentence correctly.

1. [   ] People in Finland are proud of their cultural industry.

2. [   ] Finland's cultural industry is significant in terms of its speed of expansion.

3. [   ] Television broadcasting is administered so as to prevent its exploitation by the government.

4. [   ] Book publishing in Finland is large industry in terms of the number of publishers and books published.

5. [   ] The Finns like to devote their time to learning the Swedish language by reading Swedish literature.

Complete the outline notes below. You can look at the passage if you want.

CULTURAL INDUSTRY IN FINLAND

1 Overview of Finland
- filled with green forests, sparkling lakes, and old castles in the
  1   Circle ← "Suomi"
- thriving cultural industry ← people's pride

2 Cultural industry in Finland
- definition: a distinct collection of successful and/or profitable
  2
  dealing with the culture of a given area or country
- thriving in Finland ∵ - have 3   for a long time since
  1700s
  - an increase in 4   time (esp.
  2000-2005)
  * greater than 5   industry in the northern area

3 Top three industries
1st place: newspaper publishing
  ← over 100 6   nationally

2nd place: broadcasting
  radio   on national level
  television   on local level (∵ public desire for
  7   )

3rd place: book publishing
  - 600 8   societies
  (book publishing companies)
  - world's largest per capita 9   until the 1980s
  - alive Swedish language 10

WRITING AND DISCUSSION

Read the questions below and write down your answers. Exchange your ideas or opinions with your classmates. Use the hints if you want.

1. What do you think is the pride of your country?

Hints ➡ humility / safety / proud of

Your Ideas

....
....
....
....
....

2. What do you think is a popular cultural industry of your country?

Hints ➡ cartoons / Japanese cuisine / recognized as

Your Ideas

....
....
....
....
....

FURTHER STUDY

For further study, access ActeaBo and review today's lesson.

http://acteabo.jp

Cord Blood

WARM-UP QUESTIONS

Discuss the questions below with your classmates.

1. Do you still have your umbilical cord?

2. What do you know about stem cell therapy?

VOCABULARY 🔊 16

From the choices below, choose the word which fits best in each sentence.

1. My younger brother was suddenly curled up in a _____ position on the floor.

2. The _____ cord is cut just after the baby is born.

3. Substances can travel from the mother to the fetus via _____ transmission.

4. Illegal logging is responsible for much of the _____ of rainforests.

5. Excess consumption of sugar can lead to _____.

6. The price quoted is _____ of tax, which will be added separately.

7. I used to love going to baseball games, but I _____ watch any sport these days.

8. A _____ of the population is in favor of immigration reform.

9. The trade _____ led to worsening relations between the two nations.

10. Although I failed the entrance exam, I take _____ in the fact that I tried my best.

comfort	destruction	diabetes	dispute	exclusive
fetal	majority	placental	rarely	umbilical

Summarizing (2)

It often takes time to summarize each paragraph of a passage. Instead, you can summarize it by simply writing down keywords or underlining them. Summarize each paragraph below by writing down keywords.

Example

Many people think of sharks as evil, man-eating monsters that hunt innocent swimmers down to attack and devour them. This image is far from the truth, however, and has largely been constructed by Hollywood movie producers who use this false impression to add an element of fear and danger to their movies.

In fact, many shark species are not predators at all, but are scavengers who feed on already dead prey. Out of over 470 shark species, only four have been involved in a significant number of fatal attacks on humans: the great white shark, oceanic whitetip shark, tiger shark, and bull shark. These four huge, powerful species are capable of inflicting serious injuries on their victims. However, these species usually avoid contact with humans as we are not a part of their natural diet. The average number of fatal shark attacks per year is about four, and if you compare this to the number of sharks killed each year by humans — over 100 million — it is the sharks who should be scared of us, not the other way around.

	Keywords
Paragraph 1	Sharks, hunt swimmers, movies, false impression
Paragraph 2	not predators but scavengers, avoid contact with humans

EXERCISE

Try to take keywords of two paragraphs below and summarize them.

We have all heard of shy people before, but what about a shy plant? As crazy as it may sound, one actually exists. It is called *Mimosa pudica*, from the Latin word meaning "sensitive plant." It is also known as the touch-me-not.

The *Mimosa pudica* is native to South and Central America. It is a creeping annual or perennial herb, which means that it slowly expands across any surface it is attached to. However, its real claim to fame is its strange reaction to being touched. If someone touches the leaves, they immediately fold up. This gives people the impression that it is more an animal than a plant.

	Keywords	Summary
Paragraph 1		
Paragraph 2		

>> newborn baby

READING PASSAGE 17

Read the passage below and summarize each paragraph below by writing down keywords.

1   Most of the debate around stem cell therapy involves the use of fetal stem cells, which require the destruction of human life/potential in order to obtain them. This moral dilemma is obvious, but another, lesser-known disagreement surrounds the stem cells obtained from umbilical cord blood—the 75 ml of

5 blood that remains in the umbilical cord and placental tissue after the birth of a baby. It seems that this controversy centers on whose interests the cord blood should serve: the donor's or the public's.

2   Umbilical cord blood is rich in stem cells that can be used to create any type of blood cell. While these lower-level stem cells are far from the ultimate

10 stem cell (they are not the totipotent cells that can become any cell in the body), they have already demonstrated usefulness in treating Type I Diabetes and some types of heart and central nervous system problems.

3   The theoretical limitation of using one's own stem cells is that

15 any genetic disorder that a person has will also be present in the saved cord blood, making it useless for treatment. Even though this is true, it has still provided some assistance

20 in some cases. Also for consideration is the fact that when researchers are investigating cord blood stem cell treatments for any particular problem,

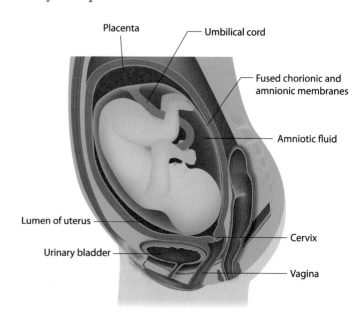

Placenta

Umbilical cord

Fused chorionic and amnionic membranes

Amniotic fluid

Lumen of uterus

Cervix

Urinary bladder

Vagina

children with their own privately stored blood are chosen first.

25 The great advantage is that the body will recognize the blood as its own, and no rejection problems will result.

⌃ obstetrician

4 While the medical establishment is always in support of donating blood for public use, it has generally voiced opposition to saving cord blood privately for the exclusive use of the donor.

30 This is because only a tiny percentage of private cord blood ever gets used, because it is rarely needed by the individual. However, a large need for it exists throughout the world, so the vast majority of privately stored blood is wasted when it could be used to help others. Private collection and storage of cord blood

35 costs a modest fee, even for lower middle class families. Public donation of it is free, though availability of the option still seems to be rare. The dispute will likely continue for decades about whether it is better to store umbilical and placental blood for one's self or donate it for the needs of others, but one can take

40 comfort in knowing that it is still an allowable personal choice.

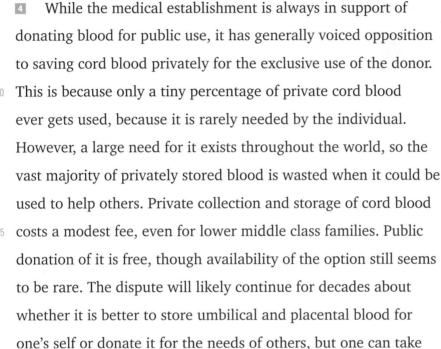

COMPREHENSION QUESTIONS

Decide if each statement is true [T] or false [F]. If it is false, write the sentence correctly.

1. [   ] The moral dilemma of stem cell therapy is that it can possibly involve the destruction of human life.

2. [   ] Umbilical cord blood can be used for treatment of some diseases including heart problems.

3. [   ] Researchers select their own children's stored blood to examine the effect of treatments.

4. [   ] Lower middle class families can store cord blood privately at low cost.

5. [   ] The debate over the use of cord blood will be completed within three years.

GRAPHIC SUMMARY

Complete the outline notes below. You can look at the passage if you want.

CORD BLOOD

1 **Debate over cord blood**

- stem cell therapy = use of **1** _____ stem cells
- obvious **2** _____ dilemma: potentially destruction of human life
- lesser-known dilemma: stem cells from umbilical cord and **3** _____ tissue from new-born baby
    - → its controversy focuses on whose advantage: donor's or the **4** _____

2 **Usefulness of cord blood**

- umbilical cord blood = create **5** _____ type of blood cell
    - → show usefulness for Type I **6** _____
      some heart and central **7** _____
      system problems

3 **The investigation**

- any **8** _____ disorder
    - → making cord blood useless for treatment
    - ← still provide some assistance in some cases
- researchers use **9** _____ with their own privately stored blood
    - → the advantage of no rejection

4 **Public vs private use**

- for public use
- for **10** _____ use
    - ← opposed by medical establishment
    - ← rarely used by the individual and wasted

UNIT 1

UNIT 2

UNIT 3

UNIT 4

UNIT 5

UNIT 6

UNIT 7

CORD BLOOD   UNIT 8

UNIT 9

UNIT 10

UNIT 11

UNIT 12

UNIT 13

UNIT 14

WRITING AND DISCUSSION

Read the questions below and write down your answers. Exchange your ideas or opinions with your classmates. Use the hints if you want.

1. Do you want to spend money on storing cord blood for private use? Why?

    Hints ➡ suffer from / be cured

    Your Ideas

    ....
    ....
    ....
    ....
    ....

2. If you have a baby, would you agree to donate your baby's cord blood? Why?

    Hints ➡ convince / understand the effectiveness

    Your Ideas

    ....
    ....
    ....
    ....
    ....

FURTHER STUDY

For further study, access ActeaBo and review today's lesson.

http://acteabo.jp

57

UNIT **9**

Author's Purpose and Tone

Graffiti: From Graffiato to Hip Hop

WARM-UP QUESTIONS

Discuss the questions below with your classmates.

1. Have you ever seen works of graffiti art? Where and what are they?
2. What artistic works are impressed on your memory?

VOCABULARY   CD 18

From the choices below, choose the word which fits best in each sentence.

1. The walls around the station were covered in colorful _____.
2. Police arrested the boys for _____ after they broke several windows.
3. If the weather is good this weekend, let's make an _____ to the beach.
4. The cows and sheep were _____ peacefully in the fields.
5. _____, or selling of sexual services, is prohibited in the majority of cities.
6. My father _____ a hole in the door for the new lock.
7. The gangster gained _____ through his many crimes.
8. Great _____ exists between the US and Canada in the sport of ice hockey.
9. Italy is known for its _____ expensive sports cars.
10. Many homeless people are living in _____ shelters under bridges.

chiseled	excursion	graffiti	grazing	incredibly
infamy	makeshift	prostitution	rivalry	vandalism

Author's Purpose and Tone (1)

An author always has a goal in mind when (s)he writes something. The goal might be (a) to provide the reader with information, (b) to argue a point, or (c) even just to make the reader laugh. To achieve this goal, the author will adapt the vocabulary and the information presented, affecting the tone of the article.

Example

What do you do when you get a headache, toothache, or fever? Well, if you go to the doctor, there is a good chance that he or she will give you medicine with at least some aspirin in it. Aspirin is a drug that has become more and more popular because it can help people with many ailments. Today about 40,000 metric tons of aspirin are consumed each year, and it has become one of the most widely used medications in the world.

Most people use aspirin as an analgesic to stop pain. Therefore, most headache tablets and painkiller medicines have aspirin in them. It is also used as an antipyretic to stop a fever. Many cold and flu medicines also have aspirin in them. Moreover, small amounts of aspirin taken every day can help prevent heart attacks, strokes, blood clot formation, and even cancer. It does this by making the blood thinner, so the blood can move around the body more easily.

Is aspirin dangerous? Does aspirin have side effects? Aspirin is a drug, and like any other drug, it can be quite dangerous. Several hundred people die each year from taking too much aspirin.

	Example answer
The author's tone	(a) to provide the reader with information

EXERCISE

Read the first or two paragraph page on p. 60 and understand author's purpose and tone.

The author's tone	Your answer
First Paragraph	
Second Paragraph	

≫ graffiti

READING PASSAGE 🎧 19

Read the passage below and understand the author's purpose and tone.

 Many people around the world have thought of graffiti as being illegal vandalism, and laws are enforced in many places to prohibit this activity. What most do not realize, however, is that graffiti has been around for a very long time, as far back as prehistoric times, taking the form of illustrations of
5 wildlife and hunting excursions scratched onto the walls of caves. From there, messages containing personal concerns, such as where herds were allowed to graze, mourning someone who had passed away, remarking about marauders, and even advertising prostitution have been found chiseled out on boulders and stone walls in the Middle East, dating back to the first century BC.

10 **2** The origin of the word "graffiti" comes from the Italian word "graffiato," which means "scratched." These scratched-out signs and symbols give us hints about past civilizations and their way of life. Taking a closer look, you might find that not a lot has changed in human nature in all of these years, for those who have taken to the streets as modern-day graffiti artists have also had the
15 mission of getting their communication across to the masses.

3 Many graffiti artists have gained infamy, but the originator, the Father of Graffiti, is "Cornbread," the artistic name for writer Darryl McCray. In Philadelphia in 1967, he began his legendary "tagging," which in graffiti

« graffiti zone in Taipei, Taiwan
(cc by Everlong)

» "approved" graffiti in
Germany
(cc by Kai Hendrik Schlusche
Lörrach Germany)

vocabulary means painting your name in your own style of letters on city
20 buildings, train cars, and buses. This act of painting one's name—and/or
artwork or messages—in public places has spread to every corner of the world
and become a cultural phenomenon.

4   Graffiti is now thought of as a vibrant expression of hip hop culture,
along with rapping and street dancing. This creative environment has been
25 credited with helping to reduce inner-city gang violence by replacing it with
artistic battles of graffiti and dance. The graffiti battles may sometimes have
political or local rivalry themes, but they are safe, alternative ways for artists
to express themselves. Some can be appreciated as incredibly detailed sorts
of masterpieces. An example of the value of graffiti artists and their art today
30 is shown by the fact that some cities have designated places for such art and
have gone through the trouble of installing makeshift walls, put up especially
for graffiti expression, which can later be taken down or moved.

COMPREHENSION QUESTIONS
*Decide if each statement is true [T] or false [F]. If it is false, write
the sentence correctly.*

1. [　] The oldest form of graffiti took the form of illustrations of
   animals and hunting.

2. [　] We gain hints about foreign cultures and ways of life from
   scratched signs and symbols.

3. [　] Darryl McCray began his artistic style of tagging to become a
   worldwide legend.

4. [　] Graffiti battles serve as a way for people to express
   themselves without exposing themselves to danger.

5. [　] Some works of graffiti artists are highly evaluated and
   contribute to the attraction of some cities.

UNIT 1
UNIT 2
UNIT 3
UNIT 4
UNIT 5
UNIT 6
UNIT 7
UNIT 8
UNIT 9
UNIT 10
UNIT 11
UNIT 12
UNIT 13
UNIT 14

GRAFFITI: FROM GRAFFIATO TO HIP HOP

Complete the outline notes below. You can look at the passage if you want.

GRAFFITI

1 Its history

- 1 _____ vandalism and prohibited by laws

  BUT

- exist for a very long time as 2 _____
    - e.g.) wildlife and hunting excursions on the walls of caves
        - = messages of personal 3 _____

2 Its features

- word origin: an Italian word "graffiato" = " 4 _____ "
- hints for past 5 _____ and their way of life
  - ≒ modern day graffiti arts : communication to
        - the 6 _____

3 The Father of Graffiti

- "Cornbread" = the 7 _____ name for writer Darryl McCray
- started "tagging" = painting one's 8 _____ in own style of
        letters on vehicles and buildings
        - → became a 9 _____ phenomenon

4 Its role

- a vibrant expression of hip hop culture
  - → artistic battle
  - → reduce inner-city gang violence
- 10 _____ as detailed sorts of masterpieces
    - e.g.) some cities designated places

WRITING AND DISCUSSION

Read the questions below and write down your answers. Exchange your ideas or opinions with your classmates. Use the hints if you want.

1. Do you agree that graffiti arts should be prohibited in your city? Why?

> *Hints* ➲ disturb the peace / art masterpiece / attract

Your Ideas

....
....
....
....

2. What do arts mean to us? Also, give an example of an opinion based on your own experiences.

> *Hints* ➲ healing / stimulate / creativity

Your Ideas

....
....
....
....

FURTHER STUDY

For further study, access ActeaBo and review today's lesson.

http://acteabo.jp

UNIT 1
UNIT 2
UNIT 3
UNIT 4
UNIT 5
UNIT 6
UNIT 7
UNIT 8
UNIT 9
UNIT 10
UNIT 11
UNIT 12
UNIT 13
UNIT 14

GRAFFITI: FROM GRAFFIATO TO HIP HOP

Author's Purpose and Tone

Human Genetic Engineering

WARM-UP QUESTIONS

Discuss the questions below with your classmates.

1. Do you want to keep your youth? Why?

2. Which of your physical abilities do you want to improve?

VOCABULARY 🎧 20

From the choices below, choose the word which fits best in each sentence.

1. The _____ of smallpox was one of humanity's greatest medical achievements.

2. Alice's _____ on the piano is incredible in a girl so young.

3. Water _____ into ice when it reaches its freezing point.

4. Mosquitoes are still a _____ to human health all over the world.

5. _____ in a gene carry the risk of causing serious illnesses.

6. Ski jumping is an _____ difficult and dangerous sport.

7. While what you said is true, that point is _____ to our present discussion.

8. I made it through the _____ stages, so now I can enter the main tournament.

9. The ultimate purpose of war is to _____ your enemy.

10. I had _____ begun to explain why I was late when my boss started yelling at me.

barely	eradication	extremely	irrelevant	menace
mutations	preliminary	prowess	solidifies	subjugate

Author's Purpose and Tone (2)

Authors have various purposes of giving readers information to make them laugh. To achieve these purposes, they will vary their tone, using, for example, an objective, favorable, or skeptical tone as appropriate.

Example

Author's tone	Example
Objective	People read many books during a long winter.
Favorable	A long winter encourages people to read more books at home.
Skeptical	People do not have any options other than reading books at home during a long winter.

EXERCISE

Read the two paragraph below and write your answer about author's tone in the table below.

Passage A

> My uncle Matt used to collect butterflies. He would catch them and display them in glass cases in his study. I was often attracted when looking at those beautiful winged insects. One of my hobbies today is watching butterflies flying free in the wild and enjoying the many patterns formed by their colorful wings and graceful flight.

Passage B

> Some people collect butterflies to catch and display them in glass cases. The author's uncle was such a person. It was amazing for the author to look at those beautiful winged insects. One of my hobbies today is watching butterflies flying in the wild and analyzing the many patterns formed by their wings and flight.

Passage	Your answer
Passage A	
Passage B	

READING PASSAGE 🎧 21

Read the passage below and try to understand author's purpose and tone.

    Manipulating genetics is considered the "holy grail" of medicine. When it is fully harnessed, everything becomes possible, including longer life and extended youth, the eradication of illness and disease, and greatly enhanced mental and physical prowess. As of now, these remain the domain of science
5   fiction; modern science is still struggling to solidify its first step: changing one gene.

   The virus has been a menace to all life from the very beginning, but what if this threat could be re-purposed to help us? This is exactly what genetic engineers are doing for people suffering from Severe Combined
10   Immunodeficiency (SCID). SCID is caused by an inherited genetic mutation, and it results in the carrier being born without an immune system. In a process called gene therapy, a certain type of virus is manipulated to make a useful change in the human genome with the outcome of producing a working immune system. SCID is an ideal
15   candidate for this type of procedure, because changing only one gene will fix it. Yet, as simple as this sounds, gene therapy also carries an extremely high risk of causing cancer. The reason it can be done on SCID infants is because SCID will cause death much earlier and faster
20   than cancer, so the threat of cancer becomes irrelevant—

⌃ DNA strands

66

any extension of life is an improvement. So far, SCID is the only disease on which gene therapy has been attempted.

3   Treating SCID is considered negative genetic engineering, because it treats a negative in order to bring an individual up to an average level of health
25 and ability. It is nearly universally considered ethical (except perhaps in the preliminary testing on animals). Positive genetic engineering, contrary to the sound of the name, is surrounded by heated ethical arguments. It has not yet been attempted, but positive genetic engineering consists of improving on a human body that is already healthy and at or above average standards. Such
30 improvements might include improving intelligence and memory, increasing athletic performance, or even increasing aggressive tendencies (for military interests). The main fear surrounding positive genetic engineering is that only the wealthy and those in government will be able to afford it, and, over time, they will become a different and superior species and subjugate the rest of
35 humanity.

4   Human genetic engineering is barely in its infancy. The power of manipulating genetics promises to change humanity forever—for better and for worse.

COMPREHENSION QUESTIONS

Decide if each statement is true [T] or false [F]. If it is false, write the sentence correctly.

1. [   ] It is considered that manipulating gene will improve our mental and physical capabilities.

2. [   ] Genetic engineers try to manipulate genes to help people suffering from an immune-related disease.

3. [   ] One type of gene therapy involves a process to control a certain type of virus to modify the human genome.

4. [   ] Manipulating genes makes it possible to extend the lives of infants suffering from SCID and treat their disease.

5. [   ] Genetic engineering could enhance intelligence, athletic performance, and aggressive tendencies.

Complete the outline notes below. You can look at the passage if you want.

HUMAN GENETIC ENGINEERING

1 Manipulating genetics

- "holy grail" = everything possible
- now: domain of science 1

   = try to 2   its first step = changing one gene

2 Gene therapy

- virus = a 3   of all life

   BUT

      re-purposed to help people with SCID

                                    = 4   genetic

                                 mutation and born

                                 without an immune system

- manipulating a certain type of virus to make an 5

   change in human genome

- SCID = an ideal 6   ← fix by changing only one gene
- carry a high risk of causing cancer

   e.g.) done on SCID infants to 7   their life

3 Negative vs Positive

- negative: bring an individual up to an average level of health and

      ability

- positive: 8   on human bodies

   (* already healthy and at or above average level)

      - its fear = only the wealthy and those in government

         9

4 To the future

- human genetic engineering: barely in infancy
- the power: promise to change 10   forever

UNIT 1
UNIT 2
UNIT 3
UNIT 4
UNIT 5
UNIT 6
UNIT 7
UNIT 8
UNIT 9
UNIT 10
UNIT 11
UNIT 12
UNIT 13
UNIT 14

HUMAN GENETIC ENGINEERING

WRITING AND DISCUSSION

Read the questions below and write down your answers. Exchange your ideas or opinions with your classmates. Use the hints if you want.

1. Do you agree with using genetic engineering technology to clone humans? Why?

Hints ➡ donor / against nature / moral right

> **Your Ideas**
>
> ....
>
> ....
>
> ....
>
> ....

2. What do you think will happen in the future if human genetic engineering is developed?

Hints ➡ ruin of mankind / artificially / cure any diseases

> **Your Ideas**
>
> ....
>
> ....
>
> ....
>
> ....

FURTHER STUDY

For further study, access ActeaBo and review today's lesson.

http://acteabo.jp

Dr. Martin Luther King, Jr., a Man of Passionate Callings

WARM-UP QUESTIONS

Discuss the questions below with your classmates.

1. Who do you respect? Why?

2. What words or phrases have encouraged you most?

VOCABULARY 22

From the choices below, choose the word which fits best in each sentence.

1. People used to believe that seeing a comet in the sky was an _____ of misfortune.

2. Keith felt very angry, but _____ he displayed no emotion.

3. The Internet opened up new _____ in human communication and interaction.

4. Mozart was a _____ boy when he began to write symphonies.

5. The Second World War was a _____ event in world history.

6. A _____ is a person who studies religion.

7. If I can _____ you that I am telling the truth, will you help me?

8. One aim of _____ in the US was to open up all schools and colleges to black people.

9. A great _____ can inspire many people through his or her words.

10. The government _____ legislation to give women equal pay to men.

convince	desegregation	dimensions	enacted	mere
omen	orator	outwardly	pivotal	theologian

Making Inferences (1)

An inference is a thought process — also called a "deduction," "conclusion" or "interpretation" — that you carry out when you learn about a subject. Making an inference while you read means that you are making this presumption, even though it is not stated clearly in the text. An inference helps us understand what is expressed "between the lines."

Example

> If you visit the town of Roswell in the US today, you will still find people arguing about what really crashed in that farmer's field back in 1947. You will also find a UFO museum that helps keep the story alive.

Inference	• Some people believe that a UFO exists, while others think it is a hoax.
	• The story of the UFO has been discussed for a long time.

EXERCISE

Read the sentences below and infer the meanings.

> There are over 15,000 species of butterflies in the world today. Unfortunately, that number is decreasing. Their declining population is due to pollution and loss of habitat.

Inference	

⌃ King with
President
Lyndon
Johnson in
1966

READING PASSAGE 23

Read the passage below and infer the meanings.

1   Martin Luther King, Jr. is known as the most celebrated of American activists of the 1960's Civil Rights Movement. It must have been an omen when his father changed their names from "Michael" King to "Martin Luther" King after the Protestant leader and initiator of the Protestant Reformation,
5   for his life grew to be one of passionate callings with an outwardly displayed courage to answer them.

2   Martin Luther King, Jr. became a Baptist minister in 1954. After graduating from Crozer Theological Seminary, he earned a Doctor of Philosophy degree from Boston University. It was the beginning of a well-
10   thought-out life, but it became a subsequent realization that there had been a dimension of great purpose and urgency about it when that life was taken at the mere age of 39.

3   What brought on the events which led to this pivotal point? It stemmed from relationships with influential people with like minds, attitudes, and
15   beliefs. One was Howard Thurman, an educator, civil rights leader, and theologian at Boston University, who taught King the non-violent activism ideals of Mahatma Gandhi. King visited Gandhi himself, later stating, " . . . I am more convinced than ever before that the method of non-violent resistance is the most potent weapon available to oppressed people in their struggle for
20   justice . . . "

4   In 1957, Dr. King helped found the Southern Christian Leadership Conference (SCLC). The SCLC organized and led marches for desegregation (which is the liberation from any law or practice that would require those of a

« King at a Civil Rights March on Washington, D.C., 1963

» Martin Luther King was greatly inspired by Gandhi.

« King is most famous for his "I Have a Dream" speech, given during the 1963 March on Washington for Jobs and Freedom.

25 particular race to be separate from those of other races) and worked for blacks' voting rights and labor rights. During the "March on Washington for Jobs and Freedom" in 1963, Dr. King delivered his famous speech, "I Have a Dream," at the Lincoln Memorial in Washington, D.C., making him one of the most inspiring orators of all time.

5 In 1964, Dr. Martin Luther King, Jr. was awarded the Nobel Peace Prize
30 for leading non-violent opposition against racial prejudice in the United States. As a result of the Civil Rights Movement, the US Civil Rights Act of 1964 and the 1965 Voting Rights Act were enacted into law.

6 On April 4, 1968, while standing on the balcony of his motel in Memphis, Tennessee, where he had been supporting black public works employees, Dr.
35 Martin Luther King, Jr. was shot and killed by an assassin. Conspiracy theories have emerged but with no definite conclusion. A day earlier, he had delivered his "I've Been to the Mountaintop" address saying, " . . . we, as a people, will get to the promised land."

COMPREHENSION QUESTIONS
Decide if each statement is true [T] or false [F]. If it is false, write the sentence correctly.

1. [   ] The father of Martin Luther King, Jr. asked a religious leader to name his son.

2. [   ] Gandhi taught King the principles of non-violent activism, which were developed by Howard Thurman.

3. [   ] King believed that nonviolent resistance was the most powerful tool for people who were oppressed.

4. [   ] King's speech in Washington, D.C. about blacks' voting rights and labor rights caused a race riot.

5. [   ] It is uncertain whether King's assassination was planned by a group of people.

Complete the outline notes below. You can look at the passage if you want.

PROFILE OF DR. MARTIN LUTHER KING, JR.

1 Who is he?

- American activist of 1960's Civil Rights Movement
- changed his name to "Martin Luther" King, Jr.

  ← an **1** _____ of becoming a passionate calling

2 What did he do (until 39 years old)?

1954   a **2** _____ minister

after seminary   earned a Doctor of Philosophy degree

3 What inspired him?

- Howard Thurman: the non-violent **3** _____ ideals of
  Mahatma Gandhi

- Mahatma Gandhi: non-violent **4** _____
  = most potent weapon

4 What did he do (between 1957 and 1963)?

1957   helped found SCLC

               marched for **5** _____ and worked for

               blacks' voting rights and **6** _____ rights

1963   "March on Washington for Jobs and Freedom"

      7 _____ a famous speech: "I Have a Dream"

               (most inspiring **8** _____)

5 What changed?

1964   awarded the Nobel Peace Prize for non-violent

        9 _____

Civil Rights Movement → the US Civil Rights Act and
                        the Voting Rights Act

6 His death

April, 1968   shot and killed

a day earlier   his speech = "I've Been to the **10** _____ "

WRITING AND DISCUSSION

Read the questions below and write down your answers. Exchange your ideas or opinions with your classmates. Use the hints if you want.

1. Why do some people discriminate against other people who are different from them?

    Hints ➲ cultural and religious differences / afraid of / superior

    > Your Ideas
    >
    > ....
    > ....
    > ....
    > ....
    > ....

2. What power do you think a speech has?

    Hints ➲ move people's hearts / learn wisdom /
    lead a better life

    > Your Ideas
    >
    > ....
    > ....
    > ....
    > ....
    > ....

FURTHER STUDY

For further study, access ActeaBo and review today's lesson.

http://acteabo.jp

Making Inferences

The Liberty Bell, a Very Significant Symbol

WARM-UP QUESTIONS

Discuss the questions below with your classmates.

1. What is a landmark of your town or your university?

2. How do you feel when you see the landmark?

VOCABULARY   🎧 24

From the choices below, choose the word which fits best in each sentence.

1. The current Japanese _____ was written shortly after the Second World War.

2. Traditionally minded people usually dislike _____ art.

3. Death penalty _____ want to make punishment more humane and victim-oriented.

4. The Statue of Liberty bears a famous _____ welcoming poor people to America.

5. The large earthquake was _____ by many small tremors.

6. July 4th is a date _____ in American history as marking the country's independence.

7. The bell in the church _____ to call people to the religious service.

8. The coronation of Queen Elizabeth II in 1953 was a _____ day in British history.

9. Before the treaty becomes law, it must undergo a _____ process in parliament.

10. Without _____, it is impossible to achieve anything important.

abolitionists	avant-garde	constitution	hallowed	inscription
momentous	preceded	ratification	tenacity	tolled

Making Inferences (2)

Making an inference is different from picking up what is clearly stated in the passage. However, you cannot make an inference simply guessing without any clue. Effective inferences require you to link the information stated in the passage with your background knowledge.

Example

Rob Coulter worked in South Africa as a game ranger. One night, while camping alone, Rob felt something hit his arm. He did not think much about it, but a little later, his arm began to ache.

The points for inferences	Your writing
The information stated in the sentences	- Rob felt something hit his arm. - His arm began to ache.
Background knowledge about it	When some wild animals or insects bite, your arm aches.
Your inference	He was bitten by a wild animal or insect.

EXERCISE

Read the sentences below and infer the meaning by connecting the information stated in the sentences and your background knowledge.

Soccer is widely considered to be the most popular sport in the world. One boy was enjoying watching his favorite soccer team with his father. Suddenly, his father and other fans of their team got angry when they saw a "red card." The boy did not know what had happened.

The points for inferences	Your writing
The information stated in the sentences	
Background knowledge about it	
Your inference	

« Nelson Mandela
(1918–2013)

» the Liberty Bell in
Liberty Bell Center

READING PASSAGE 25

*Read the passages below and infer the meanings by
connecting the information stated in the sentences
and your background knowledge.*

1 On the Fourth of July, 1993, the United States'
Independence Day, Nelson Mandela told the Philadelphia
Inquirer that the Liberty Bell is "a very significant symbol for the entire
democratic world." Indeed it is, for over one million people visit it each year
5 from countries all over the world to reflect on it.

2 The history of the bell actually dates back to 1751 when it was ordered
to celebrate 50 years of the State of Pennsylvania's original constitution. The
constitution's author was William Penn, an Englishman who was the private
landowner of the territory that became the colony, and later the state, of
10 Pennsylvania. It was called "The Charter of Privileges," and it was true to
its name, for Penn was avant-garde in his thinking, taking a liberal stance
on Native American rights, religious freedom, and the inclusion of citizens
in lawmaking. It speaks of freedoms and rights that are valued by people
everywhere. These ideals were what gave the Bell its long-lasting meaning.
15 Furthermore, it gained more value when abolitionists of slavery appropriately
adopted it as their own symbol.

3 The inscription on the Bell, taken from the Bible's
Old Testament Book of Leviticus, is, "Proclaim liberty
throughout all of the land unto all the inhabitants
20 thereof LEV XXV X." The line preceding the words,
"proclaim liberty," is, "and ye shall hallow the 50th
year," making it especially perfect for the 50th year
anniversary celebration.

4 Measuring 3.7 m around the bottom lip, the
25 Bell weighs an impressive 943 kg. Its "character" is
its crack, and there are many stories to explain it.
Most are in agreement that it had been there for years

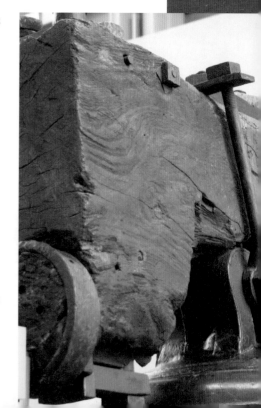

» detail of the
bell's mount

>> William Penn (1644–1718)

⌃ The Liberty Bell replica in front of Union Station in Washington D.C.

as just a thin line but widened after an enthusiastic ringing on George Washington's birthday in 1846.

30 In its history, the Bell tolled on many momentous occasions, including the ratification of the US Constitution and at the deaths of Presidents John Adams and Thomas Jefferson, both on July 4, 1826.

5 The Liberty Bell is an icon that, although
35 owned by the City of Philadelphia, Pennsylvania, speaks to all oppressed peoples, for it symbolizes the very essence of freedom—not only of speech and movement, but also of spirit. It fosters in all people a love of independence that is filled with the
40 tenacity and pride that are the strength of liberty.

COMPREHENSION QUESTIONS

Decide if each statement is true [T] or false [F]. If it is false, write the sentence correctly.

1. [   ] William Penn acquired private land which was already part of the state of Pennsylvania.

2. [   ] The Bell was considered more important after abolitionists of slavery made it their symbol.

3. [   ] The inscription on the Bell made it a perfect symbol of the celebration of its 50th year anniversary.

4. [   ] It is believed that the crack in the Bell grew larger after it was rung on the deaths of presidents.

5. [   ] The Bell encourages oppressed people to overcome their difficulties to achieve freedom.

THE LIBERTY BELL, A VERY SIGNIFICANT SYMBOL

Complete the outline notes below. You can look at the passage if you want.

THE LIBERTY BELL

1 As a symbol of US Independence Day

- July 4th, 1993 : "a very significant symbol for the

  entire 1 _____ world" by Nelson Mandela

  ↓ to 2 _____ on it

- Now _____ : over one million people visit from all over the world

2 Its history

- 1751 : celebrate 50 years of the State of Pennsylvania's original

  3 _____

  - called "The Charter of 4 _____ "

  - freedoms and rights are 5 _____ by people everywhere

    → gave the Bell its 6 _____ meaning

  : abolitionists of 7 _____ adopted it as their symbol

3 Its inscription

- taken from The Bible's Old Testament Book of Leviticus:

  " 8 _____ liberty" and "ye shall hallow the 50th year"

  → a perfect anniversary celebration

4 Its present features

- 3.7m around the bottom lip and 943 kg

- its 9 _____

- tolled on momentous occasions

  e.g.) ratification of the US Constitution and the death of

  Presidents John Adams and Thomas Jefferson

5 As an icon

- symbolizes the very 10 _____ of freedom

UNIT 1
UNIT 2
UNIT 3
UNIT 4
UNIT 5
UNIT 6
UNIT 7
UNIT 8
UNIT 9
UNIT 10
UNIT 11
UNIT 12
UNIT 13
UNIT 14

WRITING AND DISCUSSION

Read the questions below and write down your answers. Exchange your ideas or opinions with your classmates. Use the hints if you want.

1. What kind of symbols have you seen? What do they symbolize?

> *Hints* ➡ prefecture / Olympic symbol / represent

Your Ideas

....

....

....

....

....

2. Why do you think symbols are necessary?

> *Hints* ➡ feeling of security / an abstract concept

Your Ideas

....

....

....

....

....

FURTHER STUDY

For further study, access ActeaBo and review today's lesson.

http://acteabo.jp

Freedom House

WARM-UP QUESTIONS

Discuss the questions below with your classmates.

1. What is freedom for you?

2. When do you feel that you are limited in your actions?

VOCABULARY   26

From the choices below, choose the word which fits best in each sentence.

1. The prime minister _____ his opposition to the proposed education reforms.

2. It would be better to _____ a lawyer before signing this contract.

3. James has graduated from medical school and is _____ qualified to work as a doctor.

4. The _____ of women's rights is still a problem in many parts of the world.

5. New companies in the IT field can receive government _____ to help their business.

6. Before the bank can give you a loan, you have to _____ how the money will be used.

7. Once we have _____ your proposal, we will get back to you with our response.

8. It is a _____ to say that you value your health but never do any exercise.

9. In order to travel on this train, you must have a _____ ticket.

10. The cruise ship was _____ and carried thousands of passengers.

consult	contradiction	gigantic	grants	hence
proclaimed	scrutinized	specify	suppression	valid

Critical Reading (1)

Critical reading does not necessarily mean being critical of what you read. It mainly involves analyzing and interpreting the material. When you analyze and interpret the material, you apply certain reasons, evidence, theories, etc. that result in enhanced clarity and comprehension.

Example

Swaziland is a <u>small, landlocked country</u> in southern Africa. It is currently

what you can analyze ▶ limited profits from a primary industry

grappling with several big problems. About 70% of the country's population

<u>lives in poverty</u>.

high unemployment rate

<u>Droughts, floods, and other natural disasters occur very frequently.</u>

harsh natural environment and/or lack of environmental improvement

<u>Disease is also a big problem</u> such as HIV/AIDS. As a result, a typical Swazi

lack of medical services

person has an expected life span of just 50 years.

This is far below the world average of 70 years. The reason for such a bad

situation in the country lies also in that it is world's last remaining

<u>absolute monarchy.</u>

very bad political situation

EXERCISE

Read the sentences critically below and analyze them.

Although the Bushmen were hunter-gatherers for millennia, starting in

the 1950s they were forced to become small-scale farmers. As a result, the

Bushmen started a long-running court case against the government.

Free
Partly Free
Not Free

READING PASSAGE 27

Read the passage critically below and analyze them.

1   *Freedom House is an independent and non-governmental organization that supports the expansion of freedom in the world.*

—Freedom House

2   This is a simple, and yet profound, definition. What it does not tell you
5 is that Freedom House proclaims something unique to other organizations:
it is a central place to find answers about liberty all around the world. What
a valuable tool to have in our complicated world! As such, it is consulted
regularly and has hence become highly influential.

3   Freedom House was initiated in 1941 by George Field, who teamed up
10 with anti-Nazi groups and Wendell Willkie, a US Republican presidential
candidate, to start Freedom House in opposition to Adolf Hitler's center of
propaganda, the "Braunes Haus." After WWII, Freedom House worked against
anti-Semitism and the suppression of human rights. It calls itself "America's
oldest human rights group."

15 **4**   Freedom House is controlled by a Board of Trustees who have
included writers and professionals from business, law, academia, the press,
government, and labor. It receives financial backing with grants from the US
State Department, the US Agency for International Development, and the

governments of the Netherlands, Ireland, the UK, Norway, and Australia, along
20 with donations from individuals and private foundations.

5 Freedom House's yearly report, *Freedom in the World*, measures the level
of political freedom and democracy in all countries, specifying what "score"
each is given on a scale of 1 (the most free) to 7 (the least free). The scores
are put into a rating system that ranks nations as being "Free," "Partly Free,"
25 and "Not Free." The study began in 1973, and it continues to be used by many
researchers.

6 Some writers have indicated that Freedom House holds a philosophy
that includes using American economic and military strength to bring human
rights and democracy to other countries. Others have written negatively about
30 its support of political changes in other countries which are advantageous
to America. If you were to scrutinize its history and past Trustees, you might
find that it has been an organization of contradictions. Nevertheless, Freedom
House does make a valid contribution by supplying important information to a
worldwide society.

35 **7** Because of Freedom House and its annual study, the citizens of the world
receive the gift of education. It is just one step toward the understanding of
how each of us fits into a gigantic puzzle of governments and their directions.

COMPREHENSION QUESTIONS

Decide if each statement is true [T] or false [F]. If it is false, write the sentence correctly.

1. [ ] Freedom House has regular meetings and helps broaden freedom all over the world.

2. [ ] George started Freedom House together with people who worked against Nazism.

3. [ ] Freedom House is financed by donations from individuals and private foundations.

4. [ ] Freedom House analyzes and reports the level of freedom in the world every year.

5. [ ] Some writers say that American economic and military power have strengthened because of the contribution of Freedom House.

Complete the outline notes below. You can look at the passage if you want.

FREEDOM HOUSE

1 Its definition

- = an independent NGO to support the **1** _____ of freedom all around the word
- a central place to find answers about **2**

2 Its beginning

- 1941 : started in **3** _____ to Adolf Hitler's propaganda, the "Braunes Haus"
- after WW II : worked against anti-Semitism and the **4** _____ of human rights

3 Who controls?

- controlled by a Board of **5** _____ including writers and professionals from a variety of fields
- receives **6** _____ backing from
    - some US government agencies
    - governments of the Netherlands, Ireland, the UK, Norway, and Australia
    - individuals and private foundations

4 Freedom report

- yearly report: **7** _____ the level of political freedom and democracy
    : specifies "score" by a scale and a **8** _____ system
    : began in 1973 and continues now

5 Indication from writers

- positive : using American economic and military strength to bring human rights and **9** _____ to other countries
- negative : supporting political changes in other countries which are **10** _____ to the US

WRITING AND DISCUSSION

Read the questions below and write down your answers. Exchange your ideas or opinions with your classmates. Use the hints if you want.

1. Suppose you were to measure the level of political freedom and democracy of various countries today. What score would you give them on a scale of one to seven?

   Hints ➡ right to vote / limited to

   > Your Ideas
   >
   > ....
   > ....
   > ....
   > ....

2. How do you help people who are oppressed in the workplace or at school?

   Hints ➡ recommend some facilities / administrative offices / fundamental problems

   > Your Ideas
   >
   > ....
   > ....
   > ....
   > ....

FURTHER STUDY

For further study, access ActeaBo and review today's lesson.

http://acteabo.jp

Radio Frequency Identification

WARM-UP QUESTIONS

Discuss the questions below with your classmates.

1. What kind of social problems are there that need to be solved?
2. Can you give some examples of technology that makes our lives more convenient?

VOCABULARY 🎧 28

From the choices below, choose the word which fits best in each sentence.

1. In many countries, pet owners are obliged to _____ microchips in their cats and dogs.

2. Science fiction movies usually portray the world in a _____ way.

3. The mechanic explained to me that a part of a _____ is broken in my car.

4. _____ radiation includes radio waves and visible light.

5. The company holds a _____ on its new invention to protect its ownership rights.

6. We see many _____ in the media every day, such as WHO, NATO, and ASEAN.

7. Being surprised, the horse made a huge _____ over the high fence.

8. The temperature was so high that I began to feel _____.

9. Landline telephones for personal use have largely been _____ by mobile telephones.

10. Mary let out an _____ cry of happiness when she was offered the job.

acronyms	circuit	dizzy	electromagnetic	embed
futuristic	involuntary	leap	patent	supplanted

Critical Reading (2)

In critical reading, you can also evaluate the material more deeply with your background knowledge after sufficient analysis and interpretation.

Example

What you analyzed ⇨ What you deeply interpreted

In the middle of the Nevada desert, tucked between a former nuclear test site and an Air Force base is a remote piece of land known as Area 51. <u>The US government has never officially recognized the existence</u> of Area 51,

> only unofficially recognized by the people ⇨ government's secret

and <u>until recently, it did not appear on maps of the region</u>.

> now appears on maps ⇨ because its use has complete

It is not possible to walk or drive into the site, and for many decades, planes could not fly overhead.

EXERCISE

Read the sentences critically below and analyze them more deeply.

Cloud computing will revolutionize business. Before, companies always

had to operate their own Internet networks. Lots of money would go

into upgrading hardware and software in order to keep up with modern

technology. But cloud computing offers these companies an appealing

alternative. The future of computing will be determined not inside your

desktop, laptop, or even your tablet but up in the clouds.

≪ small RFID chip compared to a grain of rice

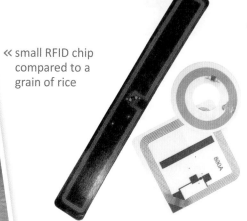

≪ RFID tags used in libraries: square book tag, round CD/DVD tag and rectangular VHS tag (cc by Grika)

≫ Léon Theremin (1896–1993) (cc by Guisan01)

READING PASSAGE 29

Read the passage critically below and analyze them more deeply.

1 Radio frequency identification (RFID) is the use of an object, or "tag," for the function of tracking and identification using radio waves. Simple research of RFID technology makes it seem limitless. From determining the winners of races to animal
5 identification (with chips embedded under the animal's skin) and passport monitoring, we have just begun to see its potential. One possible function has brought a wave of resistance, however, as the futuristic implications of monitoring humans via embedded tags have been imagined, although to date, the occurrences have
10 been limited.

2 Most RFID tags contain two parts: a small chip with integrated circuit for regulating RF signals, keeping and maintaining information (up to 2,000 bytes of data), and other various purposes and the antenna for accepting and sending
15 signals. All RFIDs are active (having a battery and transmitting independently), passive (having no battery and needing an outer point of supply to cause signal communication), or BAP (battery assisted passive).

3 There are several key moments in the history of RFID. In its
20 earliest form, an IFF (identification, friend or foe) transmitter-receiver was invented in the UK in 1915, which later allowed

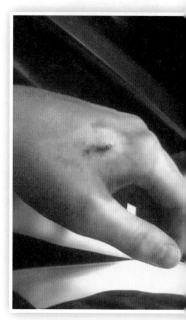

⌄ RFID chip implanted in human (cc by Amal Graafstra)

≫ sheep with an RFID tag (cc by John Haslam)

 » EPC RFID tag used by Walmart

» logo of the anti-RFID campaign by German privacy group digitalcourage (formerly FoeBuD)

Allied forces in World War II to identify aircraft. Such technology is still used today. Then, in 1945, Léon Theremin designed a spy device that is considered to have been the beginning of RFID engineering. Based on the IFF, it was made for the Soviet Union, and it acted as a secret listening system operated by electromagnetic waves. Finally, Mario Cardullo patented the first real RFID device in 1973, though the acronym RFID would not be used until 1983 with a different patent.

4 RFID technology has grown by leaps and bounds since the days of Mario Cardullo. It is gaining use in allowing touch-free payments, from waving credit cards in front of readers to paying for a dizzying number of services with a wave of your cell phone (if you are in Japan). Still, the primary use of the technology today is in supply chain management, because it improves inventory tracking, both for higher efficiency and theft prevention. Also, there is a rapidly increasing number of RFID tags utilized in electronic toll collection on highways around the world.

5 Currently, there is a field of study growing alongside the technology which is engaged in the ethics of its use. Still, the day may be fast approaching when the fear of a bar code tattooed across our foreheads is supplanted with the fear of an involuntary microscopic chip embedded in our skin.

COMPREHENSION QUESTIONS

Decide if each statement is true [T] or false [F]. If it is false, write the sentence correctly.

1. [   ] We may be able to make use of RFID to discover a new type of animal.

2. [   ] Aside from active and passive types of RFID, there is also a mixed version.

3. [   ] Léon Theremin, the first inventor of RFID, made a secret listening system.

4. [   ] The main use of RFID today is touch-free payment by credit cards and cell phones.

5. [   ] IRF technology is used to prevent theft of commodities.

Complete the outline notes below. You can look at the passage if you want.

RADIO FREQUENCY IDENTIFICATION

1 What is it?

- the use of a "tag" for 1 _____ and identification using radio waves

- see 2 _____ in: determining the winners of races
  - animal identification
  - passport monitoring

2 Its features

- 2 parts : a small chip with integrated circuit for regulating RF signals, etc.
  - : an antenna for accepting and sending 3

- 3 factors 1. 4 _____ : have battery and transmit itself
  - 2. passive: no battery and need outer point of supply
  - 3. BAP: battery 5 _____ passive

3 Its history

1915 in UK	the earliest form of RFID invented
	(used to identify aircraft in WWII)
1945	the beginning of RFID
	(6 _____ as a spy device for the Soviet Union)
1973	the first 7 _____ for real RFID device
Until 1983	the acronym RFID not used with a different
	7

4 Where is it used?

- 8 _____ payments : waving credit cards or cell phones
- supply chain management : 9 _____ inventory tracking
- ETC on highways

5 Its future

a field of study for 10

WRITING AND DISCUSSION

Read the questions below and write down your answers. Exchange your ideas or opinions with your classmates. Use the hints if you want.

1. What do you think of implanted microchips under people's skin?

   Hints ➲ verify identity / at one's own responsibility

Your Ideas
....
....
....
....
....

2. What do you think will happen if RFID technology improves?

   Hints ➲ read one's identification / separate / deny

Your Ideas
....
....
....
....
....

FURTHER STUDY
ActeaBo

For further study, access ActeaBo and review today's lesson.

http://acteabo.jp

UNIT 1
UNIT 2
UNIT 3
UNIT 4
UNIT 5
UNIT 6
UNIT 7
UNIT 8
UNIT 9
UNIT 10
UNIT 11
UNIT 12
UNIT 13
UNIT 14

RADIO FREQUENCY IDENTIFICATION

Tips for Reading: Reflecting on your study

Now that you have completed this textbook, how much have your English abilities improved? On Page 7, you set your goal and smaller steps. How many steps have you taken now?

Now is the time for you to stop and reflect on your learning.

- How much have you achieved?

- Was your method of learning OK?

- Is there anything you should change? If so, how?

LET'S TRY

Reflect on your English learning.

Your original goal	
Your original smaller steps	
How much you have achieved	
Things to change	